eh?

by the same author

★

KELLY'S EYE and other plays

eh?

by Henry Livings

A Spotlight Dramabook

HILL AND WANG • NEW YORK

Eh? was first produced by the Royal Shakespeare Company at the Aldwych Theatre, London, on 29 October 1964, with the following cast:

PRICE	Donald Sinden
ALY	David David
MRS MURRAY	Brenda Bruce
VALENTINE BROSE	David Warner
REVEREND MORT	Nicholas Selby
BETTY DORRICK	Patsy Byrne

Directed by Peter Hall
Designed by John Bury

CHARACTERS

ALY: gentle Pakistani, slim and small built, earnest, dignified, and friendly. He wears an astrakhan hat, tight creased dark suit, paper-thin shoes and a white overall coat which is several sizes too large for him.

PRICE: stocky and aggressive, a hale fifty. The works manager, soberly and well dressed, he wears a small hard bowler hat which represents him well: small and hard. He likes grinding and unfunny dirty jokes, is almost devoid of humour. He can add up and he gets his own way, which is more or less his total contribution to the general good. He thinks of himself as something of a wag and jolly and friendly with it, but his emery will and self-interest keep a yeast of doubt in his dealings with others, so that his voice, for instance, comes out toneless; and his dialogue is punctuated by nasal and unmusical 'er's' in case anyone should interrupt and possibly even get topside of him. In anger, he smiles.

MRS MURRAY: a handsome and mature woman, even pretty. Professional and crisp in manner usually, she can be warm, but she tends to use her femininity. She wears a clinical overall at work, carefully adjusted to show no evidence of any clothes underneath. She's the personnel officer, in which role she has something of a struggle for recognition.

VALENTINE BROSE: is pale and totally lacking in human fire. He behaves excitedly on occasion, even frenetically, and he wears gaudy cheap clothes with some dash; but he himself stays still and unaffected in the core of the fireworks. It's as if he were giving a performance of some character he's dreamed up, and his pale eyes wander in search of effect even in his apparently wildest moments.

REV. MORT: a tough and easy-mannered man, handsome and healthy. It would be hard to say which title he prefers, father or padre, but he seldom gets either and he's humble enough to accept parson cheerfully.

BETTY DORRICK, later MRS BROSE: Val's fiancée, a bit unsure of herself, just slightly hysteric, so that she talks stridently and gets mixed up with Val; things which wouldn't happen if only she could be sure she's the buxom and pretty girl she really is.

Act One

A boiler house. Immense, spotless. Two large tubes descend from above, leading the coal first vertically, then inwards at an angle, to the turning bars which feed the two fire-boxes. The concave face of the boiler faces us with dials and valves stemming from it indicating steam pressure, phasing and speed. To one side is a spartan two-tiered bunk, a steel locker and an internal telephone extension.

On the other side of the room is the door. PRICE, *the works manager, stocky and aggressive, stands centre, looking upstage towards the bunks.*

Musak musak musak.

As the TANNOY *gives out a message, he turns his head to listen.*

TANNOY 1. This is the last call from your Shunday nat shaft vice. Good mor . . . This is the last call from your Sunday night shift voice. Good morning, everybody.

Time signal.

TANNOY 2. Good morning, everybody; welcome to friendly Monday! Night-shift figures are just coming in, but they already look GOOD! Dispatch can look forward to a hectic day, but never mind, boys, blame the dyers and that's what we're all here for. (*Solemn.*) I have a message here from the bleach croft: Bleach croft say will all workers look out for a black cat, or may be white. Thank you.

PRICE *moves over to the bunk, contemplates a bundle of blanket, and leans over.*

PRICE (*loud and clear*). Idle runt!

After a pause the occupant of the bunk whips back the blanket with an appalling scream, shoots off the bed and legs it for the door.

Aly! Aly, it's a bad dream! You're still asleep; it's all right!

ALY opens the door, which causes the sound of one bar of 'Chanson du Matin', and disappears.

MRS MURRAY comes in. Smart, mature, she carries a card folder from a file.

MRS MURRAY. Have you explained to him that you're taking him off the job?

PRICE. I think he's got an inkling.

Another scream comes distantly, and ALY comes drumming in again. 'Chanson du Matin' as the door is opened and closed. ALY hurtles back to the bunk and lies down as before.

ALY (*calm and still*). Oh, good morning, Mr Price. You will never conceive that I have had the most dreadful of dreams.

PRICE. Who'd a thought?

ALY gets up sedately, tidying his clothes. He checks the gauges and puts ticks on a time-sheet hanging attached to a board by the boiler.

ALY. Good morning, Mrs Murray. Yes, I dreamed I had a very severe welcome from you for being absent from my duties.

PRICE. Fancy. You have trouble sleeping nights?

ALY. Not at all, thank you.

PRICE. Perhaps you'd like a change?

ALY. No, thank you, Mr Price, I'm very happy: pip-pip (*Gesturing to the* TANNOY.) I press the buttons zrum-zroom tidy about pip-pip at a later date I oil oil check all gauges pressure and the needs of the dye-shed and bleaching departments by means of the telephone, and also record my experience on the time-sheet.

PRICE. Very poetical. Well, hear me: You bloody lazy slob,
no more zrum-zroom for Aly; shovel-shovel as from tonight,
up there, in the 'oppers.

ALY. Alas, I am no longer an aristocrat among workers, pressing buttons.

PRICE. That's right, alas alack you're shovelling slack. Tonight.

ALY. I shall not protest. It is all the fault of permitting the
authority of women in spheres of men. Observe this when
you fall, too, Mr Price; lovely women are for the tender
cherishing of men, there cannot possibly be enough tender-
ness in dyeworks for the proper employment of ladies. Good
morning. (*He goes. 'Chanson du Matin'.*)

MRS MURRAY. Isn't he delicious ?

PRICE. He's a walking take-over bid, that one. D'you know
he's saved over three hundred quid since he's been with us ?

MRS MURRAY. What's wrong with that ?

VAL *comes in diffidently. 'Chanson du Matin.' Smart cheap
clothes, glacé shoes and a hell of a haircut.*

PRICE. He's only earned two-fifty. I thought he'd better toil a
bit before he retires to the Taj Mahal. (*Sees* VAL.) What the
hell's that ?

MRS MURRAY. Not yet, Mr Brose.

VAL *goes out again. 'Chanson du Matin.'*

VAL (*outside*). Sorry, Mrs Murray.

MRS MURRAY. Now Mr Price, I want you to show a little
human sympathy for once . . .

PRICE. What is it ?

MRS MURRAY. It's your new – I mean he's your new boilerman. You may remember you did ask for one . . .

PRICE. Then what's he doing here at this time in the morning ?

MRS MURRAY. He wants to interview you personally – be
interviewed by you personally, Mr Price, and I beg you just
to accept that from me. Just say a few kind words. He's

rather nice. I think you'll take to him, if you give him a chance . . .

PRICE. *Take* to him?

MRS MURRAY. . . . find him a useful workman, I really don't know why I'm going through with this, but he's quite an unusual young man and you are rather overwhelming . . .

PRICE (*to stem the torrent*). Mrs Murray.

MRS MURRAY. . . . quite overwhelming. (*Nobly.*) You must understand that it takes a good deal of understanding to understand that you *can* be very understanding. (VAL *peers in. 'Chanson du Matin.' She has a touch of hysteria.*) Not *yet*, Mr Brose!

PRICE (*wonderment*). I think I'd better have a glance at this.

MRS MURRAY. References, and he's brought references . . .

PRICE. What the dickens do I want with references for a boiler-man?

MRS MURRAY. Well, they might give you some idea of his character and capabilities, but I dare say you won't want to go into that. I'm not attatall sure that you'd like the ideas involved.

PRICE (*looks at her strangely*). No. I won't. I want a boilerman, pure and simple.

MRS MURRAY. I think you may rely on me for that.

PRICE. Mm? (*Shouts.*) Come in here, you!

MRS MURRAY (*murmurs to herself*). Pure and simple.

VAL *comes in. 'Chanson du Matin.'*

PRICE. You're looking for a job.

VAL. . . . Er, yes?

PRICE. Yes?

VAL. Yes. Well, that's the first bit over, isn't it? I'm not very certain of myself, you see, can't always guarantee to come up with the right answers . . .

MRS MURRAY (*hastily*). This is Mr Price, Mr Brose, the works manager.

PRICE. Can you press a button?

VAL (*prompt*). Yes.

PRICE. No hesitation about that?

MRS MURRAY. I think Mr Price is ribbing you there a little, Mr Brose . . .

PRICE. . . . because that's about all there is to this job, an idiot could do it. (*Grins.*) This is a place for lazy operatives this is, mechanized from end to end.

VAL. No work?

PRICE. Just buttons. The only people that toil here are me and the man trimming the coal up there in the hoppers, and we sweat. (VAL's *head swivels to one side and then up to look up, then down again.* PRICE *waits.*) Anything else done here is a doddle.

VAL. Sounds all right.

PRICE. It is. It's a treat. What's Mrs Murray all nerves about with you?

MRS MURRAY. I think we can say that concludes the interview, Mr Brose.

PRICE. Well, Mr Brose? (*Leers at* MRS MURRAY.)

VAL. Oh, I don't know, I expect she was just anxious I should make a good impression. I told her I couldn't quite place myself, you know, felt more like waiting around in case I turned up . . . (*He loses the thread for a second . . . taps his foot with nervous impatience.* PRICE *watches.*) . . . than going, seeing about work, and having to talk to people that mightn't have any sympathy with my pattern of reactions. You get some right clods.

PRICE. Are you some kind of a nit?

VAL. Erm, yes, I think so.

PRICE. That gear, for instance, you'd a fooled me if you'd said you'd left your guitar outside.

VAL. I came, didn't I? Oh, I don't mind you calling me a nit, that's all right. That is, I don't mind so long as I get the post. Of course, if I don't I'll half-murder you.

PRICE (*stares*). You what? (*He turns to draw* MRS MURRAY *to one side, gazing vaguely at* VAL, *who continues calmly.*)

VAL. I'll get you, don't you worry. Some night when you're going for your bus. Scuffle, then clunk. There won't be much blood to speak of, just an agony and an aching, and not being able to drag yourself along the wet pavement.

PRICE. Your idea is I should employ this? (MRS MURRAY *contemplates* PRICE *serenely.* '*You thought you could cope, eh?*') I suppose I can be thankful there aren't too many of his sort.

MRS MURRAY. All men are a challenge, Mr Price.

PRICE. They may be to you, Mrs Murray – in fact, I can well imagine it – but this one's a dare.

MRS MURRAY. I think it'd be braver to send him packing.

PRICE (*chews his nails*). D'you think I go the wrong way about it?

MRS MURRAY. You see the result.

PRICE. I thought I'd met 'em all. He's not a nit, he's a nutter. Nothing like this ever happened to me in my whole life. At least, I don't think it did.

MRS MURRAY. How d'you know it isn't the beginning? There's a new force moving in people these days.

PRICE (*furtive glance at* VAL). Doesn't look too forcible to me. Of course, there was that one I found loading ten hundred-weight of boiler-coal into his mini . . . he had a few harsh and unnecessary things to say. I'll call the police, confront him with a copper, a copper with him; point him out. Then they'll remember him.

MRS MURRAY. Go ahead.

PRICE. I wonder if they'd remember him? Well, what can I say to him?

MRS MURRAY. Oh, you men, you're so un*sure*.

PRICE. You don't think I should be unsure? With him? (*Opens and shuts his mouth.*) You just . . . walked up to me . . . as if it were the most natural thing in the world . . . and proposed I should employ *him*!

MRS MURRAY. If you remember, I suggested, with some dif-
fidence, that if you wanted a boilerman, *if* . . .

PRICE. Pure and simple, that's what I said, I remember the
exact words.

MRS MURRAY. Yes, they sounded a bit off to me as well . . .
If that was what you wanted, I recommended Mr Brose and
I said that it would be as well if you showed some small
interest in his welfare, accepted him for what he is.

PRICE (*getting shirty*). Now you listen to me, you . . . (*Speaks
up to* VAL.) and you, c'm here, come on.

> VAL *comes over.*

VAL. Big, isn't it?

PRICE. I want you to listen to this: this is not a game, you
know, this is an industrial concern this is; nor it isn't some
kind of an atom model in a psychological laboratory, with
little coloured balls to show where all our lovely personalities
are balancing each other off so beautiful. (*Face aggressively
close to* VAL'*s.*) You'll treat me right, you will: here, right
here, is where the person finishes and the work begins. (VAL
about to face to exit. PRICE *grabs him back.*) You see? *He*
understands what I mean.

VAL. Oh. Have I got it?

PRICE. I'm going to give you a chance Mr – er – Brose, a trial.

VAL. A trial?

PRICE. A trial period.

VAL. I want to show respect to you, Mr Price, you see I'm very
concerned about my normality, but if it's to be a trial
period . . . (*Stops.*)

PRICE (*trying to keep up the pressure*). Yes?

VAL. You see, I'd be nervous and mess up things.

MRS MURRAY (*sotto to* PRICE). You've had every indication
that

VAL.   ⎫ I'm ⎫
          ⎬   ⎬ not a very stable character.
MRS MURRAY. ⎭ He's ⎭

PRICE (*examines* VAL *in detail*). A chimpanzee could do what I'm going to ask you to do, Mr Brose . . .

VAL (*smirks*). I know what you want me to ask: why don't you . . . no, I can't, it's daft . . . oh well, all right, here goes.

PRICE (*overriding*). You could perform the entire operation with your left elbow, eyes shut and in two minutes flat.

VAL. Is it paid by the hour?

PRICE. Your *presence* will be required midnight to eight a.m. six nights a week, Sunday off. (VAL *purses his lips in a silent concentrated whistle*.) You will be paid eight pounds three and six. It will be your business to supervise this boiler, in which you will find no shred of effort is required: there's no labour in this works, only productivity: not busyness, business. (*To* MRS MURRAY.) What the devil's he whistling about?

MRS MURRAY. I'll guess he thinks he's getting eight pounds three and six for his Sunday off and he's wondering how he can wriggle out of the other six days.

VAL. No. I'll admit that did cross my mind. But I was just passing the time a bit with the whistling – well, not really whistling. (*Nonchalant*.) Little coloured balls.

PRICE (*starts away indignantly to* MRS MURRAY). I will not take on this man. I will not.

VAL. Oh yes, you will; you think you won't, but you will.

PRICE. Get on to the layabout exchange, get them to scrape the barrel.

MRS MURRAY. You don't think they have done?

PRICE. This one didn't come out of the barrel; they *found* him, while they were dusting.

MRS MURRAY. Oh, Mr Price (*Hand on his arm*.), aren't you rather generating unjustified heat? Do I catch you out over-compensating for your guilt at pushing your men about? (*Radiant*.) I sometimes think you'd dispense with a man's industrial function provided he'd stoke up your power lust without making you feel uneasy.

PRICE (*round-eyed*). It's worse than a marriage!

MRS MURRAY. Oh, that too, that too.

PRICE. Eh?

MRS MURRAY (*happily biting on the word for its juice*). Sex.

PRICE. Sex?

MRS MURRAY. Pure, unambiguous, rampant, sexual insecurity, sheathed in gleaming lust.

PRICE (*intrigued*). D'you really think so?

MRS MURRAY. Mmm.

VAL. You see, when you said little coloured balls I was completely confounded, so I thought, well, perhaps you knew the answer, so I saved it up, and then I said it.

PRICE. Am I really stuck with that?

VAL (*to* MRS MURRAY). Like when you said what was my relations with my mother, I just couldn't stop myself saying son; it came straight out. I've been wondering what the proper answer was, her being dead. Now my father, he really is a dirty old . . .

MRS MURRAY (*pinched*). Thank you, Mr Brose.

VAL. Well, he stands in the bedroom window and all the neighbours out looking and then if anyone complains he goes into his hen-run and starts clucking 'Braar-chuck-chuck'.

PRICE (*cheering up a bit*). Mr Brose, Mrs Murray recommends you for this opening, and I'm going to take a chance on you.

VAL. Thank you, sir.

PRICE (*rattling on*). You're not exactly what I had in mind; in fact, I doubt if you ever were, in anybody's, but it's up to you to prove me wrong.

VAL. Just give me the chance, sir, show me the way to go and I'll go, that's all I ask.

PRICE. You don't need me to tell you that in a firm of this importance we don't tolerate poor material.

The exchange becomes more rapid as PRICE *hastens through his formalities and* VAL *is panicked to the same pace.*

VAL. Of course not, no.

PRICE. We look after you, and we expect you to look after us.

VAL. Oh.

PRICE. Yes. Now, is there anything you want to ask me before we finish?

> PRICE *waits one split second before turning away dismissively.* VAL *is concentrating tensely.* PRICE *glances back reluctantly.*

MRS MURRAY. You remember all the information I gave you? About conditions of work? Pension scheme and insurance?

VAL. I think so. I'll tell you what it is I was wondering a bit, if I'll measure up to Mr Price's requirements.

MRS MURRAY. No, no, you mustn't think like that.

VAL. I'm not sure if I'm thinking at all.

MRS MURRAY (*hand on his arm*). You can put questions to us, you know; it's a two-way bargain.

PRICE. You'll have a contract, of course; show him a copy, Mrs Murray.

MRS MURRAY (*takes one out of the folder*). You'd better take it away and read it.

PRICE. Then sign it.

MRS MURRAY. Just that you understand the general conditions of employment.

PRICE. And an undertaking that you won't join a union.

MRS MURRAY. All that sort of negotiation is looked after by our Joint Conciliation Committee, for which you are entitled to vote, or to stand if you so wish.

VAL (*desperately*). I only want to be told what to do.

MRS MURRAY. We're human, Mr Brose; we do want to help. Can't you let us?

VAL. You give me courage, Mrs Murray, you do. I'd like to take this post, that I would, and that's coming straight out with it, no messing; I'm sure I'll get great joy in it.

MRS MURRAY (*grips his forearm warmly and confidently*). That's a man.

> VAL *clutches her and plants a huge and frantic kiss on her. He releases and stands relaxed and fond. She feels suddenly nude. Pats her hair and makes a rapid exit. Drops the folder, nearly bends to pick it up, glances back at* VAL *and thinks better of it. Goes out. 'Chanson du Matin.'* VAL *picks up the folder and hands it to* PRICE *like a speech-day prize, shaking his hand.*

VAL. There's just one thing, Mr Price: will you personally favour me and come down tonight at twelve, so I can get a good start and do you some credit straight away?

PRICE (*shouts*). Yes! (*Claps his hand to his head.* VAL *turns and hurries off.* PRICE *follows as* VAL *holds the door for him. 'Chanson du Matin.' As soon as the door is shut,* PRICE *turns round and comes in again.* PRICE *gets* VAL *an overall. This time the door music is 'The Sky At Night'.* VAL *follows to centre.* VAL *realizes that he is on the centre spot and politely moves to one side for* PRICE. PRICE *looks uncomprehendingly at the centre spot, then at* VAL, *then with some apprehension he looks above. Pulls himself together.*) There it is then, Mr Brose. (*The boiler.*)

VAL (*looks and then looks away*). Oh. Oh yes, quite big.

PRICE. I'll leave you now, and I hope you'll be very happy with us. (*Sour.*) I'm for my bed.

VAL. Us?

PRICE. Eh? Oh, the firm.

VAL. It is a steady job, Mr Price?

PRICE (*abstracted*). Er, yes. Providing you're satisfactory, I suppose you *could* settle down here. Look, I suppose it *was* you that was here this morning?

VAL. Yes.

PRICE. I've only a hazy recollection of what happened, but

from what I can remember of it I wouldn't say that satisfactory is the word to describe it; I can't quite hit on the word, but it isn't 'satisfactory', no.

VAL. I'm satisfactory all right. Always been satisfactory. All my school reports: satisfactory satisfactory satisfactory. I went to the Grammar School, you know.

PRICE. I dare say.

VAL. I did Latin. Satis meaning enough, factory meaning works: Satisfactory. Had enough of work.

PRICE (*stares at him a second*). There's just one thing.

VAL. There's just one thing.

PRICE. What little you have to do, do it.

VAL. Do it. Me?

PRICE. Oil, like the card says; check, like the card says; and switch off at the end of your shift.

VAL. End of your shift.

PRICE. Because the parson comes in at a whiff of black smoke, and reports me.

VAL. Reports me.

PRICE. It'd take a genius to get black smoke out of it, but don't.

VAL (*shakes his head*). Don't.

PRICE. And don't repeat everything I say.

VAL. And don't repeat . . . the parson.

PRICE. Now see here, if you're apprehensive about this job, as you seem to be, the least you can do is inform me.

VAL. No, I think it's that I'm mostly apprehensive about everything.

PRICE. We can make other arrangements, you know, and tomorrow morning's as good a time as any.

VAL. I quite understand that.

PRICE. Good. (*He holds up his right hand, knuckles towards his own face and wags his index finger at* VAL.) Here's the finger, as soon as I know where to put it, I'll put it.

VAL *contemplates the finger.* PRICE *looks at it himself and decides the gesture needs strengthening. He dips it, as if squashing a louse, and it's clear who he thinks the louse is.*

VAL. Only I'm getting married on Saturday.

PRICE (*it jerks out after a second*). Congratulations. Have you told her who she's marrying?

VAL. Yes, and you need something steady when you're embarking on that.

PRICE. On what?

VAL. Matrimony. And the Labour Exchange said, said . . . well, it's just this getting up in the morning. I've missed my dole for the last twelve weeks because of that. They put my time for eleven o'clock. Dirty trick.

PRICE. I see. (*Tries to shake his head clear of the miasma.*) Well, you won't have that trouble here.

VAL. No, that's what I thought. Eh – oh I see what you mean. Yes, I could go along there first thing after I've finished here, couldn't I?

PRICE. No.

VAL. No. Though I could get two cards, couldn't I? I shall want something behind me for in case I can't get up in the morning at night as well. (*Reads on the boiler.*) 'Starter button.' (*Raises a finger.*) What does it start?

PRICE (*panic*). Just a minute! (*Goes to check the gears.*) I thought you understood the work?

VAL. Work?

PRICE. Well, the workings.

VAL. Didn't you tell me it was an easy job?

PRICE. Mr Brose, if we're to go on you and I must understand each other.

VAL. An easy job, that's what you said.

PRICE. So I did.

VAL. An easy job.

PRICE. *Yes.* And one of the things you must understand is that as works manager I expect to be listened to when I'm talking.

VAL. Quite right.

PRICE. I don't require your assent to be right.

VAL. No, but you were. And I listened. I listened to what you said about it being an easy job. I heard that bit.

PRICE. Glad to hear it.

VAL. Oh, I was. Listen, Mr Brose, you said, smilingly, this is a factory for lazy operatives . . .

PRICE. Yes.

VAL. Not busyness but business, you said.

PRICE. All right . . .

VAL. And that appealed to me. You appeal to me as well; you're kindly.

PRICE (*bellows*). Thanks! Now, may I have your attention?

VAL. Yes.

> *Pause while* PRICE *tries to get back on the track and* VAL *waits patiently. Finally he takes* VAL *up to the boiler and they stand before it side by side.* PRICE *points to it.*

PRICE. It's er . . .

VAL. It's er . . . a Dadcock and Wilbin forced-drag marine boiler – er, with steam super-heat and economizer and hot-air low-ram er-um feeder oil gears every four hours gearbox every four weeks. Reg.

PRICE. Roughly, yes; you seem to have an idea.

VAL. That was just a resume off this card hung up here. That was the gist of it, anyway. Excuse me, I panicked just then.

PRICE. Just when?

VAL. Before. You know, all that you said about there being no work entailed and then you started up about work and I panicked. I panic easily, need to know where I am; you being here I know where I am, don't I? Next to you, I mean.

PRICE (*screws up his eyes to look at* VAL). I think you do. (VAL *looks* ' ?' *with polite interest.*) Panic.

TANNOY. Nearly the end of Monday and hallo to Tuesday and the night shift, here it comes: Pip-pip-pip-pip-pip-pip.

PRICE (*up a slippery slope*). We expect you to be here at five to
midnight, so that you're actually pressing that button. (VAL
goes to the button and presses it.) on the pips. (*The feeders and
the fans start up, thunderously at first.*) It's a small thing, but
we require it. (VAL *realizes that he's being addressed and
turns off the motor.*)

VAL. Sorry, I missed that bit. The noise. (*Presses the button
and the machine starts up again. He comes close to* PRICE *to
hear.*)

PRICE. It's a small thing, but we require it.

VAL *shakes his head, 'Can't hear'. Returns to the button and
switches off.*

VAL. It makes a terrible noise, that thing.

PRICE. It's a small thing, but we require it. (VAL *shifts from
foot to foot, looking anxiously at* PRICE.) This making yourself
available from eleven fifty-five.

VAL. So that I can press the button at midnight spot on.

PRICE. Yes.

VAL. Well, I did.

PRICE. Yes.

VAL. We?

PRICE. We?

VAL. We require it.

PRICE. Who requires what?

VAL (*mutters*). That's what I'm wondering.

PRICE. Start with the first bit: who's we? You mean there's
more than just you?

VAL. I should think there'd be hundreds.

PRICE. Hundreds of who? Stop it! Shut up! I don't want to
know! I'm going home. (PRICE *heads for the door.* VAL
follows close and earnest.)

VAL. I've got a confession to make, Mr Price . . .

PRICE. Oh yes?

VAL. I'm not very keen on work, Mr Price.

PRICE. Oh, for God's sake not that again.

VAL. You mustn't be impatient with me . . .

PRICE (*heavy*). I think I have explained, have I not? That the work is minimal? *Be* here, *watch* the thing, *press* the button, *oil* the bearings . . .

VAL (*nodding earnestly*) . . . every four weeks, yes.

PRICE. Every four hours! The gearbox every four weeks, fool!

VAL. That's just it, all those things, the concentration; I don't think I could keep it up.

PRICE. Oh? Oh yes? You can't keep it up now, is it?

VAL. Yes, you're right there. I don't think I want this job. Listen . . . (*An* OWL *hoots outside.*) Hear that? Right on cue, Mr Price. I shouldn't be here.

PRICE. And who, my little popinjay, had you planned should work tonight's shift? Eh?

VAL. Oh. You? I mean, weren't you planning to see me through tonight anyway?

PRICE. Mr Brose, I started work at nine this morning . . .

VAL. A bit of a chat with me; that passed the time on, I dare say.

PRICE. Besides interviewing you, if that's the name for listening to the ramblings of the ganglia you have where the rest of the race has a brain, I had, believe it or not, one or two other little jobs to do.

VAL. That Mrs Murray's a nice bit of grumble, I bet.

PRICE. I come back here, at your instance, to see you start the job, and now you tell me you *won't do the job!*

VAL. Yes, well, can't or couldn't is more like it. I thought perhaps a week's wages in lieu . . .

PRICE. What the hell d'you think this is?

VAL. Be a bit of a help to me . . .

PRICE (*shouting him down*). The Irish Sweepstake? I will not be left without a firebeater; you'll take this job, goddammit, if it's the last thing you do! I don't know what you think you're on! This is not some kind of a hurdy-gurdy fair-

ground roundabout you can jump on and off as the fancy
takes you.

VAL. Oh, all right, if you're sure you want me.

PRICE (*wild*). I'll write to the Labour Exchange! You'll never
get another job. (*Re* VAL's *remark.*) What's that?

VAL. Oh yes, I should; you write to them; I've tried to explain
to them time and again.

PRICE (*panting*). You'll do it?

VAL. As long as I'm wanted. I like to feel wanted.

PRICE. Eight-hour shift, hm?

VAL. With break.

PRICE. You get no break; you're not paid for a break; you're
paid for a full eight hours. Great heavens, how can you take a
break from doing nothing? You don't even have to clean out!
(*Points dramatically up.*) He does that!

VAL (*with ringing authority*). Who else is there?

PRICE. Eh?

VAL. There's somebody else, isn't there?

PRICE (*at a loss*). I should hope so . . . not much use getting
up a hundred and forty pounds of steam all by yourself . . .
there's fifty dyeing vessels . . .

VAL. Sorry, Mr Price, I got excited, but there's somebody up
there: listen . . . (*They listen, and we hear the scrape of a
shovel above.* VAL's *head moves sharply in response, first
swivelling to the right in a galvanic movement, then lifting
more slowly over his right shoulder, then sharply down and to
the front.*) Who's that?

PRICE. The trimmer.

VAL. We passed him.

PRICE. Yes. We passed him on our way down.

VAL (*intense*). And you'll pass him on your way up. What does
he think about up there?

PRICE. How the dickens do I know?

VAL. What's he up to?

PRICE (*with emphasis*). He's making sure the coal flows down the hoppers into the feeders regularly and evenly. That's his job. Right now he's wondering to himself why the level doesn't go down, and the reason is because the ram-feeders aren't turning, and the reason the ramfeeders aren't turning is because you haven't switched them on.

VAL. Ssh.

PRICE. Shush? Shush? You can't shush me. What for? (*While* PRICE *is waiting for an answer the* OWL *hoots again.*) How did you know?

VAL. Ah, I just did. (PRICE *puts two fingers across his brow as if he fears his brains may fly out.* VAL *shoots off to reconnoitre the room. He kneels in a corner near the door, takes out a thermometer and a lurid picture postcard, and lays them on the floor. He returns to stand by* PRICE, *then immediately shoots back to the corner and returns with the postcard and the thermometer, consulting them.*) Humidity.

PRICE. Yes?

VAL. And temperature. Dankness is all. (*Smirks.*) I reckon that spot's about it. (*Shows the postcard.*) Her bottom shows violet. Mind, pink would be better, but that's for only when it's pouring down. (*Looks up at the roof. Shakes down the thermometer professionally*.) Blue's a dead loss. (*Reads the thermometer.*) You wouldn't think it'd be that cool here. (PRICE *is gazing at the postcard.*) Dead spit of my fiancée, she is. Though not in the matter of her bottom changing colour due to humidity. Leastways not so far as I know. S'pose it could happen. Will you hold the door for me?

VAL *goes out, holding the door for a second so that* PRICE *can come over and hold it for him. 'Sky at Night'. He returns at once carrying three seedboxes which are separated by short supports. The top one is covered by a folded sack. They are clearly marked 'Mushrooms'. He puts them in the 'dank' corner.*

PRICE. Eccentric, are you?

VAL. Yes, I think so; you've nothing to worry about.

PRICE. Well? Go on. Am I to be told what they are?

VAL. Ah. Now that's something I can't do just at pres.

PRICE. I think I should know, Mr Brose, don't you?

VAL. No, that's just it, I explained; I don't think you *should* know, not just now. I think it might upset you.

PRICE (*raising his voice*). I repeat: I think I should know.

VAL (*flustered and excited*). Look here, it's not a crime to be poor.

PRICE. Did I say it **was**?

VAL. I can't help the position I'm in with regard to money; that's not my fault, understand?

PRICE. Understand? No, I don't understand – am I supposed to? It's certainly no crime to be poor; I said that. If you were to ask me, I'd say it was a crime not to do something about it if you are poor.

VAL. There you are! I didn't ask you! Backtracking off on some line of thought of your own and getting at me, I know.

PRICE. Don't you talk to me like that.

VAL. Who d'you think you are? Hectoring me. You can't have it all your own way, you know.

PRICE. Are you looking for the sack?

VAL. Since you ask me, yes! That's not the way to get work out of me, Mr Price.

PRICE. Is there a way? (VAL *opens his mouth in a fearful grimace and sticks his thumb in to pick at something stuck in a tooth at the back.*) I won't take any notice, I just won't. Now see here, you'll take this job if you've any nous at all, because if you don't, I shall hound you, *hound* you.

VAL. Hound me! Yes!

PRICE. Yes! Hound you!

VAL. Hound! Hound! Hound! Isn't that just typical, when any competent psychologist'd tell you I've got a first-class persecution complex as it is. 'Job', 'work': this morning it was 'post,' 'opening'. But different now, eh? (*Points up.*) And a trimmer to watch all my comings and goings. Threats, hectorings, and bit by bit it comes out. *Mr* Brose before, but pretty soon it'll be 'Brose', I know, and me in a mental torment to know what to call you! (PRICE *has watched this last outburst with cool astonishment and now seizes* VAL *by the shoulders and shakes him like a rag doll. He lets go.*) That's better. Thanks. Calms me down.

PRICE (*wags a finger under* VAL's *nose*). I'll tell you what I'm going to do with you: I'm going to leave you to it.

VAL. Yes, got that.

PRICE. I'm going to press this button, and leave you, to blow yourself up, if that's your fancy. (*He stands by the button.*) The alternative will be to watch the gauges, and to oil the bearings.

VAL (*screwing up his eyes to remember*). Every four hours, yes. (PRICE *presses the button and the machinery starts up. Then with a brief glance at* VAL *he marches out.* VAL *follows him hyperclose, like a double image.* 'Sky at Night.' *The door closes behind them. It opens again and they return.* 'Sky at Night.' VAL *switches off the boiler.*) So you see there's another alternative, isn't there? How d'you mean 'blow yourself up if that's your fancy'? (PRICE *goes wearily to sit on the seedboxes.* VAL *waits till the last moment anxiously.*) Don't sit there! (PRICE *leaps up.* VAL *goes to draw him away.*)

PRICE. That says mushrooms on those boxes.

VAL. Yes, doesn't it?

PRICE. And, come to think of it, I seem to remember asking you about those boxes.

VAL (*puzzled frown*). Those boxes.

PRICE. And that was when you went off.

VAL. Yes, cunning, wasn't it?

PRICE. So they're mushrooms?

VAL. Erm. No. That's the maker's name. Capitals. Capital M, capital U, SHROOMS: Mervyn Uhlrich Shrooms, seed merchant.

PRICE (*stumps upstage to above the boxes*). Why do I ask?

VAL. It's me against them.

PRICE. Why, for heaven's sake, do I bother? To attempt to find out the malodorous and futile contents of his paltry brain?

VAL. Bim bom ban on his brain pan.

PRICE (*frantic*). Eh?

VAL (*recites*).   A little bit of heaven
Fell from out the sky one day
Bim bom bam on his brain pan.

PRICE *stares hostilely at him for a second, desperately trying to fathom some sense. He goes to lift the sacking off the top seedbox, stops himself, glares at his own mutinous hands, and brandishes them frustratedly. He reapproaches* VAL, *then changes his mind and goes back to the boxes.* VAL *bursts out:*

I only want to work, Mr P. (PRICE *spins on his heel.*) Give me this one chance; only you can transform my life, which has been waste and desert so far. Don't set your face against a fellow mantle, tell me how I can blow myself up if that's my fancy. I only want a steady job. I shan't let you down.

PRICE (*very calm*). I shall be watching you, Brose; I can see through you well enough to read the writing on the wall. Don't try it on moonface, just don't: you want me to think you're an idle useless waster, don't you? Aha, and why? You want me to think I'm dealing with a half-wit. Why should that be, I wonder? Because you're not, are you?

VAL. I think half's about right, Mr P.

PRICE (*hoarse and urgent*). Don't call me Mr P. . . . Nobody puts all that flim-flam up without they've got a reason; so I'm going to keep you here, yoghort-chops, like a specimen in a bottle; and we'll see who's clever-cuts.

VAL (*uncomfortable*). There's no call for you to let suspicions grow. You have to take me as you find me; je suis faite comme ça.

PRICE. I think I've found you; yes, I think so. And I don't
entertain suspicions: certainties, Brose, certainties. (*Grim
humour.*) Instructions for blowing yourself up are on the
card. (VAL *goes for the card.*) Good night. (PRICE *presses
the button and starts the machine. He goes for the door.* VAL
*stands centre, holding the card before him; but he isn't reading it,
he's gazing into space with his lips pursed as for whistling.*
PRICE *glances back and sees this performance. He returns
close, but he can't make out what* VAL's *whistling.* PRICE
stops the machine. VAL *isn't whistling, just blowing. He continues this carry-on, contemplating* PRICE *innocently.* PRICE
nods grimly.) Hundred and forty pounds of steam maximum.
The pipes are tested up to two hundred. Over that you're on
your own. Going up, I'd guess. (PRICE *goes . . . 'Sky at
Night.' Left alone,* VAL *goes cautiously to the button. He wipes
the palms of his hands on his jacket, reaches out to press,
hesitates. The phone, which makes a noise like a dyspeptic old
motor hooter, blasts off.* VAL *presses the button and the machine
roars into action. Phone again. The noise calms a little. The*
TANNOY *gives a sharp rattle.*)

TANNOY. Calling boilerhouse, calling boilerhouse. Will the
night boilerman go to a phone, please? (VAL *hangs up the
card.*) Anyone seeing the night boilerman will they please
ask him to check his steam? Bleach croft say pressure is
well down and falling.

The phone gives its regurgitive double gurk again. VAL
*strolls to his seedboxes and looks into the top one, has a
thought and goes back to gaze up at the steam gauge. As he
looks it gives a brief hiss of steam and the dial's finger moves
tentatively round, then spins, then stops, quivering.* VAL
*cranes to see, giving little jumps on to tiptoe. He can't make
it out. He wipes the sweat out of his eyes. He gets closer.
And closer. The noise of the machine builds and it glows and
grinds less evenly. Suddenly* VAL *dashes to the seedboxes and*

carries them outside the door. Strong blasts of 'Sky at Night.'
He hurries back and finds a short ladder. Phone again. VAL
belts to it.

VAL. I can't help it!

He drops the phone, leaving it dangling and chittering; takes
the ladder and leans it against the side of the boiler; scrambles
up. He has set it too far upstage and can't see the gauge. The
room is beginning to glow redly. He scuttles dangerously down
the ladder, wipes the sweat out of his eyes with a handkerchief
and then ties it round his brow.

TANNOY. Calling boiler-room, calling boiler-room. I have a
message for you: 'Bleach croft say thank you, but there's no
need to go raving mad.' End of message.

VAL tries again to see the gauge from ground-level. No good.
He races to the ladder and places it in a better position. The
safety valve splutters and then begins to give off a ferocious
blast of steam. VAL *mounts the ladder at a fair lick and then*
straight down and then up again. He cranes across to see the
gauge. The ladder slides away, leaving him spread-eagled on
the top. He leaps to his feet and hops frantically from one
foot to the other as each hots up on the man-hole. He turns
about, strips off his jacket, toboggans down to floor-level and
dashes to get the card. It has turned brown. He runs up and
down, trying to decipher it; bangs it down on the floor like
a prayer mat, kneeling before it. Suddenly he finds the
information he needs and hurtles to the gears and flicks the
handle down.

The machine quietens down. VAL *reels to the door and brings*
in his seedboxes again. 'Sky at Night.' He staggers to his
bunk and flings himself on it, drawing the blanket over his
head. The phone drones a loud dialling tone into the night.
The dialling tone fades, the light outside changes to day, the
phone replaces itself.

The REV. MORT *comes in, vigorous, good-hearted. 'Chanson du Matin.' He looks round.)*

TANNOY (*magnified murmured aside*). No, honestly, that parson never comes round except for black smoke; if you set your trousers afire with your pipe, he's round, mentioning it. Cor cripes, it's on. (*Official.*) Seven forty-five, everyone. Calling boiler-room: Our chairman once said 'There's no one here who can't be promoted, and no one who can't get the sack.' Hint, hint.

Musak plays rhythm version of 'The Rain Comes Tumbling Down the Sky', guitar, banjo and bass. MORT, *finding no one about, scratches his neck, at a loss. He glances at the* TANNOY, *looks around to be sure there really is nobody, and then sheepishly . . . as if watching himself . . . does a little finger-jive: standing with his arms at his sides, elbows facing out, knuckles to his thighs, body rigid, he shoots out his index fingers alternately or together in a minuscule interpretation of the rhythm. As the bass player takes a 'break':*

MORT (*sings: cod Scots 'Folk' accent*).

> The reverend Alex
> The Reverend John
> The Reverend Alexander John
> Alexander
> John Forsyth
> Invented in eighteen hundred and seven
>
> In eighteen seven
> Invented a powder
> Invented a fulminating powder
>
> Bang went priming
> Bang went flints
> Bang went the guns in a brand-new way.

PRICE *comes in. 'Chanson du Matin'. Big black rings under his eyes. He stands by the door, despairing of anything good, but needing to find out what has happened during the night.* MORT *looks at him cheerfully.*

The leek and the haggis, the 'taties and the beef
Might fortify the British, and fluoride their teeth;
But fulminate of mercury and potassium chlorate
Made far more holes in Britishers than the awful muck they
    ate.

PRICE. Now don't you start.

MORT. Come, come, Price, come, come.

PRICE (*unnerved*). Well, what were you doing that for!!

MORT (*humouring him with dignity*). I was passing the time till someone came along. Don't you sometimes wonder what other people do when they're unobserved?

PRICE (*bitter*). Yes. I'm sorry, parson . . . it's just that I've had rather a black smoke bad night.

MORT. Follow my example; if you're having an uneasy night don't fight it, get up and have a stroll.

PRICE. Yes, I know. (*He goes up to* MORT.) You mustn't take any notice of me, I'm a little concerned; I hope you'll understand. I've got a new hand and he's on my mind. Well, more like neck really.

MORT (*unenlightened*). I see.

VAL *rises from the top bunk, where he has been concealed.*

MORT *and* PRICE *wait for some acknowledgement of their presence, but* VAL *takes a clipboard and records readings from the dials casually, hangs up the board and departs. 'Chanson du Matin.'* PRICE *looks sickly at* MORT. *He suddenly consults his watch. Controls himself.*

PRICE. Just stepped out.

MORT. Yes. Would that be him?

PRICE. He's new.

MORT. Oh yes.

PRICE. I don't think I'll bother looking at the time and phasing sheet, I don't think that will be necessary.

MORT. Er, good.

PRICE. Seems to have managed . . . his first night on, wouldn't you say? (*Hastily on.*) Did you come to see me?

MORT. So I did, but since the young man is new . . .

PRICE. Mmm? Yes? Well? What is it? You know you can be frank.

MORT. No, no, I prefer to say nothing. You know I've always taken a completely flexible view . . .

PRICE. View, yes.

MORT. We smoke-abaters are keen, but we don't like unnecessary prosecutions.

PRICE (*spluttering like a rip-rap*). I'd like to know just what's going on? Where are we going? Just where? It's an absolute blind alley, that's what it is.

MORT (*worried*). I think you should concentrate on the facts, they can help.

PRICE (*goggles at him*). I will, I will. I'll get 'em all off, I'll *control* 'em, they'll be mine. I'll add 'em up, that's what I'll do. And then when I've got it right I'll cross it out and put ten out of ten at the bottom.

MORT. Mr Price, for heaven's sake what on earth's the matter?

PRICE (*stares at his splayed finger-ends*). I'll get 'em all there, and then I'll have them. (*Dramatically points to the boiler.*) Look at it: a miracle of modern engineering; you could burn wet sacks on it without making black smoke! When will someone invent a man for me? How much? About twenty minutes, I'll bet?

MORT. Now, Mr Price, I didn't say it was black smoke.

PRICE. I'd like to know what else—no, I wouldn't. Big column of solid soot going straight up, I know; cost me nine pounds sixteen and three a ton plus fine. Beautiful clear sparkling night sky and the firm's profits and my bonus sticking up

into it. (*He jerks his forearm vertically twice to demonstrate.*
MRS MURRAY *comes in with her folder.*) You're sure it wasn't
anything else?

MORT. I haven't said it was anything.

PRICE. That's right, no, you haven't, and I think I prefer it
that way. Morning, Mrs Murray.

MRS MURRAY. Morning, gentlemen. I see Mr Brose's presence
is marked by his absence.

PRICE. Well, that figures. No, he isn't; he's just stepped out.

MRS MURRAY. I know he has. He's just stepped out of that
gap in the fence, and was last seen going past the time office
at a smart pace.

PRICE. Did he say anything?

MRS MURRAY. He asked the time clerk to clock him off at
eight three. Said he didn't want to claim overtime he hadn't
done.

MORT. He's a meticulous worker, is he?

PRICE. He's something. And whatever he is I'm going to find
out. (*He goes for the phone.*)

MORT. Fascinating.

PRICE (*on phone*). Hallo! (*To* MORT.) I'm going to get him back
here to do his fascinating. (*On phone.*) Yes, somebody go
down to Brose's house – the address is on the file – and get
him to come to the office; I want to see him. Yes, just gone
off shift.

MORT (*going*). Search him to the bottom, Mr Price, search him
to the bottom.

He goes. 'Chanson du Matin.'

PRICE (*hand to brow as he concentrates*). Mrs Murray, I want
your assistance.

MRS MURRAY. Yes?

PRICE. Assistance, yes. (*He takes a breath.*) Describe Brose.

MRS MURRAY. Beg pardon?

PRICE. Don't mess about. It's your job to be able to give a clear picture of the hands and staff here. Give me a picture of this one. Start with what does he look like. I've forgotten.

MRS MURRAY. I've been checking through his references. (*Nervy.*) Just as a matter of routine, you know . . . and they give a fairly consistent picture . . .

PRICE. What does he look like? Hair, start with hair. (*Aggressive.*) What colour?

MRS MURRAY. Look, Mr Price, don't think I'm not sympathetic, but d'you really want to go on with this? You're not looking my best.

PRICE. I wish no information about my appearance, it's simply that I had a restless night.

MRS MURRAY. Why don't you just leave it to me to get rid of him?

PRICE. Get rid of him? He's gone, hasn't he?

MRS MURRAY. Dismiss him.

PRICE. Ah, that's just it; the crevasse creaks open, opening . . .

MRS MURRAY (*professional*). When?

PRICE. Last night, all night. Let this one go and one by one all the other decisions and responsibilities . . . they're not firm under my feet any more, Mrs Murray, they're sliding away into a green and gritty space. Tipple tipple and over they go . . .

MRS MURRAY. You're sure it was green?

PRICE. . . . until I'm standing in the *middle* . . . not even on the edge . . . still, suspended, gliding yet still. How d' you mean, green?

MRS MURRAY. You said the space was green; blue would be more typical.

PRICE. Would it really?

MRS MURRAY. You're very disorientated sexually.

PRICE. Get away. I didn't think so; sex, eh? D'you think I ought to do something about it? Glass of cold water by the bed?

MRS MURRAY. Try to let me help, instead of regarding me as a challenge.

They're getting quite warm and close by now.

PRICE. I can feel you doing me good.

MRS MURRAY. You have very powerful drives – you must know that yourself; they can be used, or they can be abused.

PRICE (*lecherous*). Can I do it a little bit and wear glasses? (*He languorously opens the folder in her hand and extracts a paper as a dominating lover might take a cigarette from his complaisant mistress's lips, wiggling his eyebrows the while. He reads the paper.*) 'F. H. B. Frint, M.A. Oxo.' Who's that?

MRS MURRAY. Mr Frint is the headmaster of the Grammar School, the galactic initials are mostly Brose's idea. Here's what he claims is his last report. (*She hands him the report.*)

PRICE. Have you checked with Mr Frint?

MRS MURRAY. After some persuasion he admitted there had been a pupil of the name of Valentine Brose, and he went on to claim he hadn't the faintest recollection of him.

PRICE (*reading the report*). '. . . is forsaking a brilliant academic future for a career in the Foreign Office . . .'

MRS MURRAY. The erased word underneath that seems to have been 'satisfactory'. D'you want to see any more?

PRICE. After a start like that . . . d'you mean there's more?

MRS MURRAY (*consults the list in* PRICE*'s hand and then fishes in the file for more papers*). Oh yes, Mr Oliver Broad, J.P.

PRICE (*looks at the list himself*). Eh?

MRS MURRAY. His connexion with Mr Broad is indicated by two press cuttings. The first is a brief disclaimer by the editor: Mr V. Brose of 2 Holy Bones was *not* the V. Brose who was prosecuted for vagrancy as reported in yesterday's late edition. The second is a report indicating that the police

failed to establish a case against V. Brose concerning the
depositing of offensive matter in a public thoroughfare. He
seems to have been fined for obstruction somehow. Mr Broad,
J.P., is reported to have said that if he had any more of this
he would clear the court. (*She hands over the cuttings.*) Other
references include Mr V. Brose senior . . . that's his
father . . .

PRICE (*hastily*). Yes, we heard about him yesterday.

MRS MURRAY. Harry Matlock, clerk at the Labour Exchange,
and Mrs Dorrick, who's his future mother-in-law.

PRICE. Did you phone the Labour Exchange?

MRS MURRAY. Yes; nobody has the faintest recollection of him
there.

PRICE. Oh well, I suppose if he's only been going there twelve
weeks they couldn't be expected to . . . Surely *somebody*
can recollect him clearly enough to comment? Have you
tried his father?

MRS MURRAY. They're not on the phone. (*Numbly* PRICE
hands back the papers.) Don't you want to hear about the
other thirty-two?

PRICE. I think this is the bit where you help me instead of
being a challenge.

MRS MURRAY. All right then, let's add up. (*She sees the mush-
room boxes.*) What on earth's three boxes of mushrooms
doing in here, d'you think?

PRICE. Don't probe too far, but the facts are that he brought
them in last night. (*He waves his arms about hopelessly.*)
. . . So, he thinks he can grow mushrooms in a boilerhouse.
Chump.

MRS MURRAY. All right, it's another fact to add. (*She looks at
the mushrooms nervously, dismisses them with an effort and
resumes.*) We advertise for a man to do an easy job; we get
one. He goes to a great deal of trouble to explain that he
wants an easy job and we tell him repeatedly that it is an
easy job. Right?

PRICE. Er, yes. Swine.

MRS MURRAY. We ask him to tell us a little about himself, and he does so; he . . . keeps on doing so . . . he never stops. I have a thirty-page transcript of our conversation yesterday. in my office . . . sounded perfectly lucid yesterday . . . I can't make any of it out. (*She keeps her eyes on* PRICE's *face, hoping for comfort; wags the folder hopelessly.*) When I inquire if anyone can vouch for him, he brings along . . . thirty-six references. (*She blinks back tears.*) There's one from the second bird-house keeper at Belle Vue Zoo. Wouldn't you like to . . . (*Dabs at her eyes with a tiny handkerchief.*) We offer him the job and he takes it, and he does it. So obviously we both agree he has to go.

PRICE. No, Mrs Murray, you've missed out why. I now have a fairly clear idea of the progress of events, thank you very much. But *why*?

MRS MURRAY. . . . He left the job ten minutes early.

PRICE. Mrs Murray, you'll have to do a little better than that; I'll remind you I'm asking for your help. I am not going to blame a night of wretched and unquiet sleep on someone's early departure from work the following morning! This situation tends to chaos, and you chirp, about ten minutes: I want a rod of iron, I want powerful and obliterating ammunition. Something like moral turpitude or industrial sabotage at the least! And, recall, I want a full physical description. Get about it.

MRS MURRAY (*frightened*). You can't sack a man for what he looks like.

PRICE. Never you mind, madam; it'd be something concrete to go on. You can't, can you? You're being evasive, aren't you? (MORT *opens the door for* BETTY. '*Chanson du Matin.*' PRICE *shouts:*) Keep out!! Don't come in here! (MRS MURRAY *is in tears.*) Now, Mrs Murray, don't cry; I didn't mean to upset you, now did I?

MRS MURRAY. You have absolutely no right to bully me in this

way; it's quite unjustified. I perfectly understand why you
do it, and I must ask you to reverse your transferences if you
please.

PRICE. Yes, of course I will, Mrs Murray, the minute you've
explained what you mean. And I'll tear small pieces off
Brose when I get him back here.

MRS MURRAY. It may not have occurred to you, but it's a
phenomenon of the human visual memory that we find it
difficult to remember the faces of those we love.

PRICE (*stares at her*). They'll be calling for us, every man jack
of us!

MORT. Excuse me again, Price, but this young woman is
looking for Brose, who I believe is your new hand?

PRICE (*spins on him*). That's him! The very man!

BETTY. D'you all shout here?

MRS MURRAY. We have to sometimes, to make ourselves
heard!

BETTY (*bellows*). Where's my Val!!

PRICE (*pounces on her: she backs away hastily round the room*).
Aha! D'you want to tear small pieces off him? I bet you do
if you have any acquaintance with him; you'll want to rend
him.

BETTY (*backing at speed*). No, I don't. I want to marry him,
don't I?

PRICE. I'd like to help you; we could do it together.

BETTY. M-marry him?

PRICE. Stand still and be talked to! (*He turns to* MRS MURRAY.)

BETTY. I'm getting dizzy.

MORT (*ushers her smoothly out*). We seem to have chosen a
wrong moment.

PRICE. She knows something. (*He turns to find* BETTY *has
gone.*) What happened? (*Dives for the door.*) Don't you dare
explain this.

MRS MURRAY *pursues* PRICE *out and then in again.*

MRS MURRAY. As a matter of fact, it's a typical case of splitting and projection of the hated love-object.

TANNOY. Health and beauty classes are at ten.

PRICE (*to the* TANNOY). Get knotted!

TANNOY. Thank you.

Curtain

Act Two

PRICE *re-enters, gripping* BETTY'S *arm, and places her firmly centre.* MORT *and* MRS MURRAY *follow. 'Chanson du Matin.'*

BETTY. I want my Val.

PRICE. Now you stay there, you.

BETTY. Where's my Val?

MRS MURRAY. Oh, he's yours, is he?

BETTY. He is the way I look at it. Shouldn't he be?

MRS MURRAY. Oh yes, you're welcome.

BETTY. He's my fiancé. Where is he?

PRICE. He's gone, that's where he is, and he shouldn't be; he should be here. I've sent for him.

BETTY. Oh, have you.

PRICE. Yes, I have. He's coming back here to do some fascinating.

BETTY. Are you the bossy type?

PRICE. Yes. I am. Bossy, that's me.

BETTY. I wish you joy with Val then.

PRICE. I'd be glad to see some. You must tell me more.

MORT. I'll say good morning then . . .

PRICE. No. No, parson. I don't want everyone going away just when I'm getting somewhere.

MORT. I really don't see what purpose I can serve.

PRICE. No, that's right; you go, then. Shut up. (*To* BETTY.) Now, I want to hear what you know about Brose; a lot, I'll bet, eh?

BETTY. I should hope so if I'm going to marry him.

PRICE. Oh? Oh yes? Hear that, Mrs Murray? Hear that . . . no, you're a bachelor, aren't you? Mark my words, she's setting up a flim-flam. They're thick, some of them. She's not going to help me, is she heck. (*To* BETTY.) You! What am I getting so angry about?

MORT. Look here, Price, you're not putting yourself in a very good light here.

MRS MURRAY. Exactly, Mr Mort.

PRICE (*grinding*). Come not between the dragon and his wrath, Mrs Murray; nor you, Mr Mort.

BETTY (*cool*). Am I supposed to be your wrath?

PRICE. *I* am my wrath, Miss . . . Miss . . .

MRS MURRAY ('*scalpel*'). Dorrick, I believe.

BETTY. Take it from me, I won't come between it then.

PRICE. Don't, Miss Dorrick, just don't. Right, where was I?

MRS MURRAY. What does she know about Brose?

PRICE (*looks at her open-mouthed for a second*). Exactly, I was coming to that.

MRS MURRAY. I should leave it alone.

MORT. You do look a bit odd, you know.

PRICE. *Let me speak!!* (*The rest wait, resignedly mumchance. He turns to* BETTY.) What's this about you wishing me joy with him?

BETTY (*to the others*). Who's he?

PRICE. Me? I'm me, Price, that's who I am.

BETTY. Oh yes, it's all right saying that, but where are you when you've said it?

PRICE. Come on, out with it – the joy bit; I'm a bit short on joy just now. Let's hear it. How much have I got coming to me?

BETTY. Not a great lot if you carry on like this, I can tell you – raving lunatic and bossy with it. You can't push my Val around, and not with sarky either.

PRICE (*pounce*). Why not? What'll he do?

BETTY. He'll sort you out, that's what he'll do.

PRICE (*barks*). How will he do it!

BETTY (*hands on hips – with high finality*). Because, *I* shall have something to say about it if you do.

PRICE *has a sensation that he has been pierced by a sharp-edged instrument, and he daren't move for fear of worse damage. He gives a brief whimper.*

PRICE. Ah.

MORT. Mr Price *is* the works manager, you know, Miss Dorrick. I mean, it is usual for works managers to have some say in the administration of most concerns.

BETTY (*delighted*). Ooh, am't I daft? Well, you soft thing, how was I to know? Here was I thinking ooh heck what a gorilla and all the time he was perfectly entitled! Sorry, Mr Thingy. Ooh, I say though, you have to laugh though, don't you? If only to show you've got a sense of humour. That's what Val says, anyway.

MRS MURRAY (*sotto, kind and motherly to* PRICE). Shall we go now, Mr Price?

PRICE (*glassy*). Have you ever had the experience of raising a foot to mount a stair that wasn't there?

MRS MURRAY. Come along, Mr Price.

MORT. Yes, indeed; most disconcerting.

PRICE. Or tried to bite upon an apple on a string?

BETTY (*joining in the game*). Yes! Your teeth clack clack on nothing. I know.

PRICE. Ransacked a room, every cupboard, every drawer, having forgotten or having no idea what it is you seek?

BETTY (*whisper*). He's got a lovely sense of humour, hasn't he?

MRS MURRAY. Be a man, Mr Price. I understand. Don't let it destroy you.

PRICE. Have you ever, in the dawn, sought to lift the sash of a window which was open?

BETTY (*giggles*). Oh, he's right, you know.

PRICE (*turns unseeing eyes on* BETTY). Then you are a man, my son. (*He surveys their bemused faces with icy dignity.*) It's all a joke, eh? Humour, eh? I think I can safely say I am not without humour. I tell jokes. I have as much humour in me

as any . . . any . . . tin-headed maypole, who chases so
hard after a job that he nearly gets it, who (*Drawing a long
sobbing breath.*) starts work just in time for a collection for
his wedding.

MRS MURRAY (*to* MORT). He has a great many responsibilities.

MORT. Distressing. I had no idea.

PRICE. Eat the grapes, go on.

BETTY. Is he queer?

PRICE. All I said was eat the grapes; nothing queer about that.
That was in jest. Humour.

BETTY. What's he on about? My Val's done nothing wrong.

PRICE (*roguish*). What has he done?

BETTY. Nothing; he's done nothing, as far as I know. What's he
on about?

MRS MURRAY. I rather wish I hadn't come out.

BETTY. He's a good man is Val, perhaps a bit independent;
Mr Mort, you tell him.

MORT. Me?

BETTY. Well, of course; he goes to your church, doesn't he?

MORT. Oh. Oh, does he? I'm afraid I don't . . . of course,
it's a large parish . . .

BETTY. I've seen him, going in, six-thirty every Sunday
evening. You're going to marry us!

MORT (*worried*). Probably my curate . . . Look here, Miss
Dorrick, I shake hands with every member of my congre-
gation after evensong; it's a democratic gesture which, I
feel . . . it causes a certain amount of dissension, I know,
but the eye of the camel's needle is nothing to do with the
North door . . . I assure you I *know* them and . . .
and . . .

BETTY. He goes out the other door.

MORT. I don't think he does; it's normally locked at that hour.

MRS MURRAY (*eyebrows raised*). The belfry?

MORT. I think I'll go back to the vicarage now; my sister will
have prepared . . . (*Licks his lips.*)

BETTY. He's sort of dashing looking, with rather fine eyes and a rusky tusky oak-flavoured voice.

Pause.

MRS MURRAY. Well . . . that *describes* him.

MORT. I suppose it does.

MRS MURRAY. I mean it's definitely a description as such.

MORT. The eyes of love, Mrs Murray.

MRS MURRAY (*with a glance at* PRICE). Yes, we discussed that as well.

BETTY. He has a gift for words, does Val.

PRICE *suddenly crashes out an awful laugh, tuneless, mirthless.*

PRICE. He's definitely a humorist, isn't he? Well, I'm not averse to having a humorist in our midst. (*Chucks* BETTY *under the chin.*) It's not, of course, usual for unauthorized – er, persons to be allowed on the premises, but we can make – er, certain exceptions. (*Pats* MRS MURRAY'S *bottom.*) Eh, Mrs Murray? You've been letting me down, I think; this young lady would make things brighter in the office, for instance, wouldn't she? Come and have a chat with Mrs Murray; you'll find we're very pleasant here. Then come and have a longer chat with me. (*His laugh.*)

BETTY (*dance-hall simper*). I'm afraid you'll have to excuse me . . .

PRICE (*shouts*). Why, what have you done! (MORT *and* MRS MURRAY *have their eyes shut. The phone gurgles.*) Answer that Miss – er, Dorrick, let's see how you shape. (*She goes. He follows closely.*) You shape very well.

BETTY (*on phone.*) Hello? (*To* PRICE.) It's for you.

PRICE. Thank you, my dear. (*On phone.*) Price speaking. Yes, as a matter of fact I am in a good mood. Why? (*Laughs.*) Really? Well, that's the limit; at least, let's hope it's the limit. Thank you, my dear. (*Hangs up.*) What d'you think of that, eh? That fiancé of yours is quite a character, I must say; he has a flavour all his own. My secretary's quite shaken.

BETTY. What's he done?

PRICE. You'd think an older man would be a sobering influence, but the pair of them, really . . .

BETTY. Standing in the bedroom window, I bet.

PRICE. I think I'd better go and calm her down. I expect it was only harmless fun, typical of the family. (BETTY *has about-turned and speeds for the door.* PRICE *follows. 'Chanson du Matin' as the door is opened.*) Don't go, Miss – er, Dorrick! Oh well, warn that fiancé of yours that he's not the only one that can appreciate a joke! (*He lets the door fall to and turns back.* VAL *arrives outside.* MORT *and* MRS MURRAY *confer intimately.*)

MORT. What an appalling exhibition.

MRS MURRAY. Is laughter the source of fear or fear the source of laughter? I can't seem to remember.

MORT. I really don't know, Mrs Murray . . . I've heard it frightens wild animals.

PRICE. Now then, you two, no harmless fun. Remember the vicar's a bachelor!

They hasten out as PRICE *holds the door for them. 'Chanson du Matin.' As* PRICE *passes him* VAL *slips behind his back into the boiler-room.* PRICE *spins in astonishment and follows closely.* VAL *looks* MORT *and* MRS MURRAY, *who have turned back for the missing* PRICE, *straight in the eye and shuts the door on them.* PRICE *adjusts to keep directly behind* VAL. *For a moment* VAL *suspects there may be someone behind him. He swivels back.* PRICE *sways out of his eye-line.* VAL *lifts his foot, hoping to glimpse the intruder's foot.* PRICE *stands on one leg.* VAL *crosses to the steel cupboard,* PRICE *close on his heels, opens it, takes a toy rubber stamping-outfit from one pocket and a writing-pad from the other and begins furiously stamping on a convenient shelf, ripping off each page as it is stamped.*

MORT *and* MRS MURRAY *come back in cautiously. 'Chanson du Matin.' They watch* VAL *stamp on oblivious.*

MORT. Makes you wonder what it's all leading up to, doesn't it?

VAL *stops.*

PRICE (*genial*). The thing to do is to play it by ear.

VAL *stamps rapidly for a couple of sheets and then scuffles everything away. He closes the door of the cupboard and squeezes out simultaneously, so that no glimpse of the interior is given.*

VAL. You've no right to search my personal locker without a warrant.

PRICE (*to* MORT). I'm not going to ask. You find out.

VAL. I was stamping leaflets against the boss class and their lackeys.

(PRICE *broad grin*). I knew it was something I didn't want to find out.

VAL. That's where it's so cunning, you see.

PRICE. You went off shift early this morning, didn't you, you pigfaced idle irresponsible lout?

VAL. I think I need treatment.

PRICE. You just carry on and I guarantee you'll get it.

MRS MURRAY. Would you like to leave this to me, Mr Price? I think I can help him. You can see how tense he is.

MORT. Yes yes, it's apparent.

PRICE. You mean he shouldn't be?

MRS MURRAY. Well, will you leave him to me?

MORT. Alone? (*She nods.*) I think we should be close at hand.

PRICE. Brose, Mrs Murray will remain here with you for a short while. I shall expect you to respect her.

VAL. Yes, I will.

MORT. Just remember that we shall be close at hand.

VAL (*nodding*). And not do anything dirty.

MORT. Whether we're at hand or not you will not do anything dirty.

VAL. Like taking off her overall and looking at her and that.

Pause.

PRICE (*to* MRS MURRAY). Now who's tense?

MORT (*goes with a jerk*). I don't think he's serious, Mrs Murray.

PRICE (*following*). No, I'd say not. More of a joke he is. I can't wait for your report.

'Chanson du Matin.' They go outside and wait, with the door closed.

TANNOY (*after a fierce rattle*). Will the day boilerman go to the phone, please. This is urgent.

Phone belches.

MRS MURRAY. Now, shall we release our tensions?

VAL. Oh yes.

MRS MURRAY. Would you like to sit down? (VAL *sits on the bottom bunk. She sits by him. He hutches up to give her room and as soon as she's seated he hutches right back. He puts his chin on her shoulder like a faithful Pincher Doberman.*) Do you know how we release our tensions?

Pause.

VAL. Yes.

MRS MURRAY. There are several ways, all perfectly natural. Induced, as with drugs, habitual, like nail-biting . . . (*He sticks his nose into her ear and wags his head from side to side affectionately.*) . . . among others. I'm going to suggest shock release.

VAL. Mmm.

She screams loudly. VAL *springs up and then staggers away clutching the top of his head where it caught the top bunk.*

'Chanson du Matin' as MORT *opens the door and he and* PRICE *look in.*

MORT. Everything all right?

MRS MURRAY. Yes. It's perfectly usual technique for releasing neural tensions.

PRICE. She seems to be coping.

They close the door again.

MRS MURRAY. I want you to try it, Brose. (*He's glad to and does so, clutching his head.*) Rather good. Perhaps that teenie bit more physical than neural. You see, I think you're an undifferentiated schizophrenic . . .

VAL. I expect it's the sort of thing that's hard to stop when once you've started.

MRS MURRAY. Hard to stop what? I wish you'd listen to what I'm saying.

VAL. Screaming.

MRS MURRAY. . . . 'tiated schizophrenic and an evasive personality. (VAL *screams.*) Yes, that's very nice, but that's quite enough for the moment . . . and you show manifestations of primitive and sexual fantasies associated with hostility. (VAL *screams.*) Really.

She makes for the door. MORT *and* PRICE *can't wait to congratulate her. 'Chanson du Matin.'*

PRICE. Excellent, Mrs Murray. You must tell me how you go about it. I intend to dine out on this.

MORT. Is it really effective?

Scream from VAL. *She looks back bitterly at them.*

MRS MURRAY. . . . and paranoid thinking.

She goes briskly and they follow. VAL *collects his leaflets from the cupboard, goes to the door and peeps out. 'Chanson du Matin.' Shuts it again. Screams. He steps out and off. 'Chanson du Matin.'*

The light outside changes to night. VAL *comes in cautiously
. . . 'Sky At Night.' . . . He wears a large pink false
nose, quite convincing, attached by elastic. He stands centre,
facing us, and shuffles his feet until he's dead centre.* BETTY
looks in. 'Sky At Night.' New shoes, new coat, frivolous hat.

BETTY. Va-al? Val, are you there?

VAL (*mutters without looking*). Yes, dearest.

BETTY (*comes in to him*). What are we doing here?

VAL. Well, it's me really. I just came here and then you came
after. It's where I work now.

BETTY. Is it? I came here looking for you.

VAL. Yes. In a way I'm glad you did; made a difference with
me and Mr Price; he bursts out laughing now whenever he
sees me.

BETTY. What about that other, that woman?

VAL. She's off.

BETTY (*pause – she looks round*). Big, isn't it?

VAL. Yes. Oh yes. Well, as a matter of fact – quite big.

BETTY. Aren't you nervous!

VAL. Yes. Matter of fact, you're spot on there with that remark. (*Rueful grin.*)

BETTY. It's all right, really it is: I love you, you love me.
We're married; so we can be nervous or easy with each
other whichever we please. Take that nose off now, please.
(*Pause.*) We're married. Val.

VAL. Yes, Betty, I know.

BETTY. Anybody'd think you hadn't been there.

VAL. I did feel a bit . . . disembodied, didn't you? Not that
you looked disembodied; you looked more like bodied.

BETTY (*fond*). It's *over* now, Val, and it won't happen again.

VAL. Yes, that's right; very few people get much practice at
marrying, except parsons, of course.

BETTY (*mild impatience*). Ooh honestly, I'm beginning to
think I didn't read enough books. (*She brushes at confetti on*

her shoulder. This galvanizes VAL : *after a glance of alarm
at her he swoops to pick up a trail of it to the door, up-down-up.)*
Val! Whatever is it?

VAL (*mutter*). Confetti.

BETTY. I know what it is, you moonstruck flamer!

VAL. If you knew what it is, why did you ask, then? And
    don't use language to me, please. We're married now and
    I've got every right to –

BETTY (*after waiting*). Every right to what? (*He picks off a
    piece of confetti from his shoulder and shoves it furtively in his
    pocket, then begins to pick elaborately at a piece at the end of
    his nose.*) Yes? Oh, take that nose off, *please.* (*He picks
    away.*) Val! The taxi's waiting.

VAL. I expect he'll get fed up and go away in the end.

BETTY. But we can't let him do that.

VAL. Why not?

BETTY. What about our things? We're supposed to be on
    honeymoon.

VAL. Yes, well, we are, aren't we?

BETTY. Are what?

VAL. On honeymoon. I mean it's after the wedding, and that's
    when you have that sort of thing.

BETTY. Stop going on about the wedding.

VAL. You started it.

BETTY. Wasn't all that clever that you'd want to . . . what
    about our *things*?

VAL. Oh yes. You needn't worry about that.

BETTY. He'll drive off with them.

VAL. No, I put them under the hedge when I got out and that
    case of mine's your mam's and anyway there's nothing in it.
    He can have that. We'll go back and pick them up after a
    bit. I've got quite a lot of things to explain to you.

BETTY. You *what*?

VAL. I've got quite a lot of things to explain to you.

BETTY. You put them under the hedge?

VAL. What? Oh yes, the cases. (*He lopes obliquely to her, is about to halt in a suitable stance to tell her all, but continues in a loop round and back up to the mushroom-boxes, into which he gazes intently.*) You have to be very understanding.

BETTY. Well, I will; you know that. When you fell off that flagpole and broke your ankle, I didn't go on at you: I can understand anything, anything that's understandable.

VAL. Yes, that's what I mean; I'm a bit anxious about that.

BETTY. Anxious about what?

VAL. Among other things. (*He lopes to her as before, stopping this time in the stance from which he will tell all.*) This is a man's world, Betty, make no mistake. (*She looks round the boiler-room.*) What I neglected to tell you was I didn't – I forgot to book us anywhere to stay at Southport – well, more like I just didn't do it.

BETTY. But – but what are we going there for, then?

VAL. Ah. Ah, well, that's just the point.

BETTY. I wish you'd take that nose off.

VAL. No. No, let me keep it on for a moment, if you don't mind. I feel I need it. Adds a bit of gaiety to the occasion. (*Looks at her earnestly.*) At least, it would if you were to make a laughing remark, you know, like: 'Take off that nose, Val, do.'

BETTY. I did.

VAL. Yes, Yes, I know you did. But not very laughingly.

BETTY (*patience*). What are we doing here?

VAL. Well, I know what you're going to say, and I'm sure you're right if it was only practical considerations, but the fact is I don't fancy stopping with your Mam. (BETTY *closes her eyes and says a silent prayer.*) Where else.

BETTY. Where else?

VAL. Where else, yes. There you are. I told you I knew what you'd say.

BETTY (*tries again*). Val, darling Val, I really don't mind too much you forgetting to book us digs in Southport . . .

VAL. Or a hotel. I was thinking more of a hotel; a lot depends
  on a marriage getting a good start, no worries . . .
BETTY. All right then, a hotel. Anyone can forget something.
VAL. Yes, anyone; anyone can forget something. That is,
  when they set off to remember it in the first place. I'm really
  grateful to you, Betty, for that; it makes me love you even
  more.
BETTY (*gay*). Well, that's it: we can't go back home because
  I'm not letting anyone call my husband a fool, and we
  haven't anywhere booked. Answer: let's go and book somewhere. (VAL *looks at his watch and then swiftly conceals it from*
  BETTY.) I grant you the middle of the night's a bit late for
  starting looking . . .
VAL. Oh, Betty, oh, Betty, honestly you're a marvellous person.
  (*They embrace. He breaks, looks at her and then lopes off up
  to the mushrooms again tensely*.) You just have to be patient:
  that's how the good things happen.
BETTY. It's easy to be patient when you're happy: you don't
  want the time to go.
VAL. Yes. And you must be patient about this next bit, too.
BETTY. Val, the taxi's waiting.
VAL. Betty, this is a man's world here . . .
BETTY. Yes. You said that before.
VAL. And I reckon to be a man and somebody's got to be the
  master.
BETTY. Val, the taxi. (VAL *shoots off determinedly for the door*,
  BETTY *following*.)
VAL. Aye, him an all; if I can't talk to him man to man . . .
  No. (*He veers round at the same speed and back to centre*.)
  You've got to understand, Betty, that I haven't booked us
  anywhere to stay and what's more I don't fancy stopping
  with your Mam.
BETTY. You said that before.
VAL. Stop saying you said that before.
BETTY. You stop saying what you said before.

VAL. I can't; it keeps pouring out of me: if I stop I'll have to tell you what's really bothering me. I don't want you to shout.

BETTY. What's really bothering you?

VAL. We're going to live here. I've got no money.

BETTY. Of course you haven't; I've got it here, in my handbag.

VAL. Oh yes, I gave it to you for safe-keeping, didn't I? How much have we got?

BETTY. With the seventy-five in my Post Office we've got eighty pounds. Why?

TANNOY. Hallo, night shift. Welcome to nearly Sunday.

VAL. We shall need it, every penny.

> BETTY *is staring at him pop-eyed, outrage gathering in her like a tornado. For seconds she watches him. He shifts, smiles ruefully at her, leans forward for a peck, pulling the nose to one side on its elastic. Meanwhile:*

TANNOY. Just time before the pips to tell, as if you didn't know, about the Brose wedding today. Of course, it went off well, and Val is really grateful for the gallon can of liquid manure his mates clubbed up to get him. Good night to the evening shift and good evening to the night shift: here they come.

> *Time signal.*

BETTY. We . . . are . . . going . . . to . . . live . . . where?

> VAL *replaces the nose.*

VAL. You shouldn't frustrate a man's affections, Betty, my Dad said, didn't he? You want to think about these things.

BETTY (*high staccato yell*). Your Dad's a drunken lecher! We are going to live *where*?

VAL. Hush up, Betty; you're allowed a bit of nervous tension on your honeymoon, but there's no call to make a political convention of it. I grant you Dad was a bit affectionate, but he was quiet with it.

BETTY. Your Dad was quiet after he fell over on the washbowl and only after! He's got hands like gloves! Tell me again what you just said!

He goes for a glass of water from the cupboard.

VAL. What?

BETTY. It's not true. I didn't hear it. I won't believe it.

VAL. You mean about living here? I don't think I'll bother saying that again until you've sobered up – I mean simmered down. There you are, you see; you've got me saying anything now.

He chucks the glass of water in her face and returns the glass to the cupboard.

BETTY. Good God, it really is happening to me.

VAL. There you are, you see, that calmed you down quite a lot. I understand, don't you worry; I knew exactly what you were feeling, I could tell. I'm permanently that way myself, when you get to know me better . . . (*Breaks off. Does his silent whistle.*) I was worried you might shout. *He* might hear.

He stares at her, waiting rigid with anxiety for her question. She whispers it in bewilderment.

BETTY. Who might hear?

VAL (*head swivels sharply to the right and then more slowly to look upwards and then the galvanic yell comes:*) Him up there!! (*Head swivels immediately back down, slowly.*)

BETTY (*hands over her paralysed ears*). It's true, it really is. I married a maniac.

VAL. No, no, I'm not. Not exactly a maniac. I've got it all planned with fanatical thoroughness: planished steel and burmese teak, you'll see; oysters, brown or white bread, driving around in motor-cars, smiling away, twin beds with candlewick covers, non-stop variety.

BETTY. Shut up! I'm going back ('*to mother*') . . .

VAL. Cleave to me, Betty.

BETTY. Eh?

VAL. Cleave to me.

BETTY. I'll do no such thing.

VAL. You must. I'm your husband.

BETTY. Oh yes?

VAL. And anyway my Dad's let my room to Mr Thacker.

BETTY (*going*). I've still got a mother, thank heaven.

VAL (*Valentino*). Aye, there's that as well. (BETTY *stops*. '?')
I thought this could be where you could sleep. (*The bottom
bunk.*) Be a bit tricky going back to your Mam after this.
(*He moves the nose solemnly on to his forehead to look at her.
She comes slowly back to him. As she reaches him he nods,
satisfied.*) I knew you'd come back; s'funny this gift of mine.
My eyes do dominate women. (*She grasps him by the shoulders and shakes him like a rag doll. He clutches at her and
smothers her with wet kisses.*) Oooh, Betty, um um – I do
want you, Betty. (*She backs away from his leeching until
they end up with her back against the bunks.*)

BETTY. *What* about my mother?

VAL. Yes, I fancy her a bit as well. I told her and she said:
'Go on, you daft thing.' First time she's ever been civil.
(*Kisses.*) I told her would she look after my Dad on account
of his head and the washbowl and him being a widower, I
thought it'd be best; and that you didn't want to tell her
how you didn't want us to live with her after all, so I was
telling her. (*Kisses.*) I'll always tell you I love you, darling,
every day, darling, even when I've gone off you a bit. Course,
it's more carnal now, but I'll settle down honest, I know it.
(*Kisses. He puts his arms either side of her across the bunk to
grasp the other edge, and dotes.*) So Dad's to have our room.
(BETTY *bursts into floods of despairing tears. He relinquishes
her to take off his jacket, busily preparatory to donning an
overall coat.*) No, it's all right, darling; she'll forgive you in
time. (*She gets into the bottom bunk and turns her face to the*

wall. He puts on his overall.) You see, there's another thing.
A new husband always has a problem how to come to terms
with his mother-in-law. That's always one of the emotional
problems high on the list. Well, I reckon I just about fixed
that. (*He stands by the starter button.*) I know you're fed up
and far from home just now, but you've got me. (*Wail of
rage and grief from the bunk.*) There's just one other thing.
BETTY (*sobs*). Wha-at?
VAL. Don't let anybody see you here. I haven't quite got round
to asking permission yet. The right moment hasn't come up,
I don't think. (*Smirks.*) They'd have something to say.
What? I should coco. The bride in the boilerhouse. Rum.
(*Does a brief and minute jig. Pause. Contemplates the button.
Looks towards the bunk. Raises a finger.*)
BETTY (*tensed up*). What are you going to do now?
VAL. Erm. I don't know. Yes, I do. I'm going to start work;
should have been on five minutes ago, but you kept me
talking.

> *Presses the button and the fans and feeders roar into action
> accompanied by a scream of despair from* BETTY. *She draws
> the curtain across. He gets into the top bunk. The noise
> quietens.*
> *The light changes to day outside.* BETTY *gets up and gets
> two cups of tea from above the bunk. Goes back and holds
> one out just above* VAL's *chin. He gives a helpless murmuring
> groan.*

BETTY. Cup of tea.
VAL. Ank ou ery erch.
BETTY. Cup of tea, Val.
VAL. Es.
BETTY. Tea. (*Pause.*) Val.
VAL. Es . . . u i on er . . . u i own mwhere.
BETTY. Cup of tea.
VAL. U i *own* mwhere.

BETTY. Cup of tea, Val.

VAL. Oh . . . o. On't e uel 'ey. Ou ar alf otten. (*She moves the
cup closer. He feebly flaps a hand. She puts the cup into it.*)
I'll sphill i'll phill i ill.

> *He makes a very weak attempt to raise his lips to the cup.*
> BETTY *folds her arms to watch. Eases himself off the bunk
> like a string of sausages. Carefully transfers the cup to the
> other hand by poking a finger elaborately through the handle.
> Raises the cup, which droops over the finger, slopping the tea.
> Eventually he achieves a gurgle with what remains. He
> gazes vaguely at* BETTY, *mopping at his sodden sleeve.*
> BETTY *watches with detachment.*

BETTY. I expect I'll get used to the glamour of marriage; then
I'll have to make an adjustment. It's twenty to eight.

VAL (*thoughtful*). Twenty to eight. Last night or tomorrow
morning?

BETTY. Shouldn't you be doing something at that? (*The
boiler.*)

VAL. You shouldn't be here.

BETTY (*she could throttle him*). Oooh.

VAL. You'll have to go now, you will.

> *He goes over to the mushroom-crates and picks up a red
> oilcan which is on a drum of liquid manure above them.*
> BETTY *strides determinedly after him, takes his face in her
> hands and plants a kiss on him.*
> *He lays down the oilcan, wipes his hands on his trousers
> and embraces her tenderly, kissing her neck softly.*

BETTY. I knew I must have done it for something. (*She undoes
the bottom button of his shirt and pulls it open a little.*)

VAL. Well, it's the best part really, isn't it? (*He does up the
bottom button of his shirt and tucks it in.*) And yet there's
better to come.

BETTY (*undoing the next button*). Is there?

VAL (*doing it up*). Yes.

BETTY. This'll do me. (*Undoes the third button.*)

VAL. I've thought of everything. (*Does up the third button.*)

BETTY (*undoing the fourth button*). I'll bet you have.

VAL (*doing up the fourth button*). I'm thinking of everything now.

BETTY (*down to the bottom button again*). So am I.

> VAL *picks up the oilcan dreamily and draws back the sack from the mushrooms.*

VAL. Come back at eleven fifty-five. (*He squirts the oilcan into the crates without really looking.*)

BETTY. Val, what are you doing oiling those crates? If anything needs oiling, it's *that*. (*The boiler.*) Calf head.

VAL. I'm feeding my mushrooms.

BETTY (*quietly*). He's feeding his mushrooms.

> MORT *is hesitating outside the door.* VAL *goes to open the door for* BETTY.

VAL. You take your little case with you; you'll want to freshen up, I dare say. (*She opens the door. 'Chanson du Matin.'*) See you inside the Roxy usual time?

MORT. Hill-oo?

> VAL *pushes the door to, but* MORT *is peering in through the gap and is trapped by the cheekbones.* MORT *grips the door and forces it back so that between them,* VAL *leaning with all his weight and* MORT *just pushing with one hand, they maintain it open about a foot.*

May I come in?

> VAL *gestures wildly to* BETTY *to hide.* MORT *is baffled to know why the door opens so far and no farther.* VAL *plants his foot to jam the door.* MORT, *making a further effort to get the door fully open, realizes that it's at the bottom that it's stu ck He gropes round.* VAL *sets the oilcan on the floor*

and skips across to draw BETTY *up the far side of the boiler.
Holding the door with one hand,* MORT *crouches and gropes
round for the impediment. His hand lights on the oilcan, which
he picks up and examines. To his puzzlement the door is now
free.*

Hill-oo?

VAL *sets the ladder against the boiler and urges* BETTY *up
it.* MORT *enters.*

Excuse me! I just happened to be passing! (*Looks at his
watch.*) Mr Bro-ose! Ha-rum! It's me, the padre!

VAL *scuttles back to above the bunks for* BETTY's *pink overnight case.* MORT *spins at the sound. He goes to look in both
bunks.*

BETTY *reaches the top of the boiler and waits for* VAL *to
climb up and draw up the ladder for the descent on the other
side. She begins to hop as her feet hot up.* VAL *begins to hop.
She lets out an inadvertent yelp in her urgent whispers to*
VAL: *like a flash* VAL *depresses the safety valve and their
grunts, hops, yelps and scutterings are partially disguised by
the violent hissing and the clouds of steam.*

MORT *is galvanized by the sudden inexplicable activity of
the boiler and runs to the front to see what can cure it.* VAL
manages to lower the ladder and get BETTY *down it, keeping
the safety valve going intermittently the while.* MORT *grabs
the phone and shrieks inarticulately into it:*

Arc! arc! arc! Who? It's me! The padre! The parson! The
vicar! Look here, what the devil does it matter who's speaking? Send help! The vicar! V I C A R, send help! H E L
. . . H for Harry, E for Elephant, L for lion, P for it's
blowing off!

VAL *follows* BETTY *down, carrying the overnight case, and
lets her out of the door. 'Chanson du Matin.'* MORT *still on
the phone.*

It's stopped now, but by heavens if it hadn't a fat good of lot you'd have been!

> BETTY *returns to the doorway and gives* VAL *a ringing smack on the back of the neck and goes again.* MORT *hangs up and turns to see* VAL *by the door. Advances cautiously. Stops. Looks down at the overnight case.*

That's a handy little case.

> VAL *looks down at it, and opens the door.* 'Chanson du Matin.' *He hurls the case out and closes the door.*

Extraordinary. You weren't by any chance here just now?

VAL. You know how some people are liars by reservation?

MORT. Mm?

VAL. Loophole liars: they don't tell lies, not actual lying words, but you end up by not getting the truth just the same?

MORT. Oh yes.

VAL. Well, I'm one of those.

MORT. Really. I merely asked were you by any chance here just now?

VAL (*careful*). No, I was not by any chance here just now. (MORT *has an anguished moment while he tries to find the verbal snag in that one, mouthing the sentence over.*) Why, what happened?

MORT. The boiler behaved in a most extraordinary manner. I was wondering – I mean you have been attending to it? Not sleeping through or anything foolish, mm? B-because I mean four and a half minutes black smoke in the hour you are allowed by *law*, but, well, not ninety minutes – not that – not ninety or more, not at all; that's going far too far. *Were* you asleep?

VAL (*as on oath*). No, I haven't slept all night.

> MORT *goes through a slightly more unnerved version of his first anguish, thinks he's found the loophole, pounces:*

MORT. You were awake, but you weren't attending to the boiler.

VAL. No, I was not not attending to the boiler.

MORT (*after a moment*). D'you think perhaps it wants attending to? I mean, you're not actually doing anything just now, are you? You can't argue that . . . it was blowing off. I should be glad, for instance, if you could – well, oil it a bit. I should be happy to witness that. (*Holds out the oilcan.* VAL *takes it and goes over to stand by the mushrooms.*)

VAL. That's the gearbox, over there.

> MORT *looks over to the gearbox.* VAL *squirts the top mushrooms splat.* MORT *looks back at* VAL.

MORT (*suspicious*). Where?

VAL. On the left.

> MORT *looks;* VAL *squirts the middle box splat;* MORT *looks at* VAL.

MORT. The box.

VAL. Yes.

MORT. You're going to lubricate it?

VAL (*tensing up*). Aren't you interested to examine it?

> MORT'S *head flicks in that direction, but he remembers in time to prevent* VAL *from feeding the bottom box unobserved.*

MORT. No.

> VAL *fingers the oilcan nervously and then sets off at a high speed for the gearbox.*

VAL. I shall need you to open it for me, then.

> MORT *follows to help* VAL, *but* VAL *veers round and back to the seedboxes.* MORT *turns back.* VAL *is caught and stands rigid.*

MORT. Just a minute. What d'you do when I'm not here?

VAL. I don't do anything when I'm not here.

MORT. I mean who opens the gearbox . . . what's that? You don't do anything? Mm? Think twice before you answer: black smoke may be subject to a fine and I need to know which way my duty lies: have you – examine your conscience – have you in any way failed to pay proper attention to that boiler during any part of last night, Saturday to Sunday September twenty–twenty-one nineteen sixty-three?

VAL. No, I have not in any way failed to pay proper attention to that boiler during any part of last night Saturday to Sunday twenty–twenty-one nineteen sixty-three.

> MORT *chews his knuckles desperately, looking for the loophole.* VAL *squirts the last and bottom box splat.* MORT *leaps on him with a snarl and drags him roughly across to the gearbox.*

MORT. Some of you people seem to forget that the clergy is chosen from among the laity! I'm not a celluloid fiction of the community folklore. I have my full complement of human characteristics, I have. I'm a rugger blue to boot. (*Final shake.*) Don't chance your luck, Brose. (*Stares at* VAL, *panting.*) The secret dragons.

> VAL *busily hands over the oilcan to* MORT *and gets another bright yellow one from the cupboard, with which he pumps away into the gearbox.*

VAL. Oh yes, the secret – erm, dragons.

MORT (*eagerly*). You know them? You understand?

VAL. What? Oh the – er . . . No, I don't understand. (*Lips pursed in a soundless whistle.*)

MORT. What's wrong with *this* oilcan? (*The one he's holding.*)

VAL. Got no oil in it. (*On with the whistling.*)

> MORT *experimentally pumps a splat of manure on to the floor. He hands back the oilcan to* VAL.

MORT. Sorry. (*Sniffs.*) Curious smell.

VAL. It'll be the secret dragons. (*Smirks. Purses lips again.*)

MORT. Wha . . .? Or – er, yes. (*Short mirthless laugh.*) You taking the mickey?

MORT.⎫
VAL. ⎭ No, I am not taking the mickey.

MORT. Yes. But why dragons, eh?

VAL. You started it. (*On with the whistle.*)

MORT. No, listen, just listen: I'm sure there's a perfectly adequate explanation for the curious sequence of events since my arrival a few minutes ago. I'm quite sure of it. (VAL *stops his silent whistle and* MORT *has a brush of panic.*) No, don't attempt to account for it, if you don't mind; let's take it for granted . . . But it became somewhat of a nightmare for me. I know you'll laugh. (VAL *smirks obligingly.*) but it did, because I was ignorant. (*He's getting into preaching form now.*) Because I did not know. Wildly we flail our arms in the dark; no faith can protect us against our terror of the unknown. It may be the faint tap-tap of a wind-shaken branch at the window, but in our sleep-sodden consciousnesses it is menace, and we cannot believe: there is no bed, no room, no world in which we live . . . there is no God.

VAL (*anxious*). Oh yes, there is.

MORT. No faith to protect us, no God to rescue us.

VAL. Oh yes, there is.

MORT. No!

VAL. You're a fine one to be talking like this, a parson an' all.

MORT. This is the region of evil: here be dragons. But is it just that it is unknown? I don't know everybody in Halifax, but I have no fear of them.

VAL. You get some right rough uns . . .

MORT. No, it is the nameless terrors within yourself. Within. The emptiness of the animal mind conditioned and equipped only for survival, yet governed by the inexplicable *need* to

survive, which is fear. Those terrors have been pictured for
us by men we call geniuses, witch doctors, preachers, artists:
they have fabricated us dragons. But why dragons? A tiger
is a silent, savage, killing animal. A rhinoceros, the wild
African elephant, are huge, active and destructive, yet they
play walking-on parts in our dream of evil and chaos. The
dry terror of the dusty snake becomes, in our stories, the
wily serpent! The nearest creature we have to our pictured
dragons is a lizard! No lizard can inspire fear.

VAL. Glory alelluyah!

MORT. Eh?

VAL. Glory alleluyah. I'm getting with it now.

MORT (*concentrated hypnotically on* VAL). Before God created
man, before man pushed off on his two big toes and pattered
erect to chalk his slogans of divinity on the wall, there were
dragons. Before. Seventy million years ago by the stone
clock the tyrannosaurus, forty-five feet from nose to tail,
eighteen feet tall on its huge haunches, teeth like stilettos
and vestigial forelegs that wouldn't even reach his mouth.
No man ever set eyes on such a creature, not by tens of
millions of years; it's a bare hundred years since his gigantic
bones were contemplated with any understanding. And
yet . . . and yet . . . (*A great saurian roar reverberates
through the auditorium.*) . . . he *existed*. And what soft-
bellied breathing fish swerved away from the tread of those
great claws, missed the razoring of those teeth? What
smooth pellet of grey matter folded that horror in, stored
it, and thinks it *now* fishlike in the waters of a woman's
womb, still prints it off to shadow the imagination and burst
the skull of sophisticated man?

The roar again, more central. VAL *can hardly hold his
bowels together.* MORT *can see the grail.*

VAL. I believe in God!

MORT. I believe in God!

MORT. In nomine patris filii et spiritus sancti!

The roar again, forte to piano. A door swings and bangs in the auditorium. Silence. MORT *smiles on* VAL *benevolently:*

A dream of evil and chaos. Don't chance your luck, Brose. (*Sniffs.*) Curious smell, that is.

VAL (*shaken*). We're all right really, aren't we?

MORT. What a fellow you are. Of course we're all right.

VAL. Here.

MORT. Yes.

VAL. Because we're not here.

MORT. We're . . . who isn't?

VAL. Us. You said we missed them by several millions of years. I wonder who we are if it's not us?

MORT. It's very early in the morning, Brose . . .

VAL. There you are for a start: it's my bed-time. I can't believe it's clever of you to get at me. Prosecutions for black smoke and that, that I could cope with: 'Call Valentine Brose . . . Are you Valentine Brose? I am.' That's a cinch, no doubt in my mind, you bet. Valentine Brose, that's me. Guilty. But threats, and – and dragons. I mean, you do see what you're making yourself responsible for? You've been inventing rules, haven't you? And I haven't even played the game yet.

MORT (*stern smile*). Exactly, Brose: play the game.

VAL. Yes, well, all right, but which one?

MORT. You're one of these people who's against 'them', aren't you?

VAL. Oh yes, I'm against them all right.

MORT. Has it ever crossed your mind to wonder who them they are?

VAL. Is there them-theys as well?

MORT. Think about what I say: play the game. (VAL *thinks about it.*) I'm glad you used that word responsible, because you know I do feel responsible. I want you to know that.

VAL. I've been meaning to ask you if you could help me. (*He goes for the clipboard.*) I feel very lonely.

MORT. Faith can give us back our identity.

VAL. Yes, I think you're right. Can you read those dials?

MORT (*takes the board*). These what you have to fill in every shift.

VAL. Three times. Gets me down. And then my eyes are not so good and I get in some right arguments: that flipping typist reckons she can guess better than me. In the office. I have to traipse up there an' all.

MORT. Doesn't seem an impossibly difficult task.

VAL. Yes, identity, you've hit it.

MORT (*more interested in the card*). Mm? You know, industry, when you size it up, comes down to a very simple set of figures.

VAL. Those cards were good. Had one with my picture on in the army. M.P.s were always interested. Who am I if there's nobody here? (*Backs towards the door.*)

MORT. Prayer, in which we strain to merge ourselves with the Almighty Will, strangely confirms our individual worth.

VAL (*at the door*). I think I have serious withdrawal symptoms. (MORT *looks up vaguely and then back at the board.*) Shan't be a minute.

> (VAL *slips out.* 'Chanson du Matin.' MRS MURRAY *approaches and enters briskly. She is dressed smartly for Sunday, slacks, sloppy Joe and a slightly martyred air.* MORT *does a very slow double take on her, like a chicken registering a marble.*)

MORT. What happened to Brose?

MRS MURRAY. Through a hole in the fence, where else? He was wearing a false nose.

MORT. Oh.

MRS MURRAY. Shouldn't you be at church?

MORT. More or less. You?

MRS MURRAY. Couldn't sleep. Did you speak to him?

MORT. A little, why?

MRS MURRAY. I was wondering what brought on the false nose, you or me.

MORT. I should say it was spontaneous.

MRS MURRAY (*yawns*). I hope you were careful: you do realize he's got serious withdrawal symptoms?

MORT (*getting a bit funny*). Yes. Yes, and I begin to see where he got them from.

MRS MURRAY. Pardon?

MORT. Quite a little recidivist, isn't he?

MRS MURRAY. I don't follow.

MORT. I mean, he may not know the rules, but he's a fair idea where they aren't.

MRS MURRAY. It's very early in the morning, vicar.

MORT. Well, we shall just have to get up a little earlier, shan't we? It seems I have this sheet to deliver to the office; but tomorrow, Mrs Murray, you and I and Mr Price shall put our heads together, with malice aforethought. (*Smiles genially.*) We'll see who's the joky man.

He tears off the sheet and hurls the board aside, crumpling the sheet savagely. He goes out smoothing the sheet against his chest.

'Chanson du Matin.' MRS MURRAY *follows him out.*

The light outside changes to night. VAL *and* BETTY *are now concealed in the bunks, the chintz curtain drawn round the bottom one. 'Teasmade' above the bunks rings. Pause. Scrape of shovel above. Pause. Appalling scream from* VAL *in the top bunk.*

BETTY *draws back her curtain and gets herself a cup of tea. She takes the clipboard from the floor and checks the gauges, sipping her tea as she fills in the sheet. Replaces the board, and goes sedately to bed with her cup of tea, drawing the*

curtain. A mighty kick from her sends VAL *shooting off the
bunk. Bewildered, to find himself on his feet, he consults his
watch blearily.*

VAL. Must be four o'clock. (*He gets the clipboard and shuffles
about trying to consult the dials and fill in the sheet, gradually
realizing that the job has already been done. Nervous wrought-
up mumble:*) It's happening again: every time I go to fill in a
number there's one already there. (*Shakes his wrist and consults his watch. Head swivel to up and down. Groans tensely.*)
You aren't half rotten, Betty. That's the thirty-fifth time
you've done that.

BETTY (*invisible*). That's the thirty-fifth time you haven't
woken.

VAL. I don't want to quarrel with you, Betty, but it's forty-two
actually : a week before you came here and then our wedding
night, then the six weeks since, less seven Mondays off.
(*Dispirited.*) Whoopeee. (*Puts on his false nose.*) D'you know
what I think about the odd time, Betty, when I realize you've
kicked me out of bed again ?

BETTY (*invisible*). What ?

VAL. Your white thigh.

Pause.

BETTY (*invisible*). I've got two.

VAL. Yes, but I only think about them one at a time. Take
things steady. What do you think about ?

*She sticks her arm out through the curtain and waves it
about, looking for a grip on him. He contemplates it and
then turns away his gaze. His soundless whistle.
She turns over and looks out for him, gets out of the bunk
and approaches him from the back. and puts her hands round
to take hold of the nose. He places a forefinger on the
elastic either side of the nose to hold it on.*

BETTY. Guess who ?

VAL. Erm, Betty?

BETTY. Honestly, I always read about 'peek-a-boo' with newly-weds: kind of exciting to find you always and really-truly knew who it was. But it's not a bit like that with us, is it?

VAL. Did you get a reply to your letter?

BETTY. No, it just said 'Fat flustered and twenty please send a stamped addressed envelope'.

VAL. Is that what you signed yourself?

BETTY. Mm. I suppose there could be another one similar.

VAL. Flip her then – no, don't take my nose off, Betty. No, you just have to think about it.

BETTY. I'm not unhappy with you, Val; it's just that it's – well, it's unexpected, you know. I'm quite surprised. Shall we think about something now?

VAL. Okey doke. (*Pause while they think about something. Eventually* BETTY *sighs luxuriously.* VAL *looks at her hotly.*) I'm boss inside my own head. Boss. Are you pressing down your toes inside your mules?

BETTY. Yes. Wriggling them a bit, too.

VAL. So am I. More pressing than wriggling with me, though.

BETTY. Little bit of wriggling.

She reaches out sensuously, pulls on his nose and lets it go gently. Takes it off him, squeezes it in her hand until it's a rag, hands it back to him. He murmurs:

VAL. Not much, though. Eh no, Betty, give us back my nose. I'm just getting used to it; you can get used to anything in time . . . Ah, now look what's happened. (*Pockets the remains of the nose.*) You'd no business doing that.

BETTY (*cooler*). Say that again?

VAL. I've always wanted to be able to see my own nose, only I couldn't. I think it must be too small. And it's no good a mirror because the image is reversed and you don't know whether it's your right hand or your left for picking at

things. All I got before was a sort of pink blancmangey
shadow and I could never believe it was that narrow: you
try it. (*He squints down his nose as a demonstration.*)

BETTY. What was that about getting used to anything?

VAL (*increasingly nervous*). The trouble with you is you're not
interested in my desires. I tell you what, Betty, way you
behave sometimes I sometimes wish I'd married someone
with a bit more zest and passion. And sparkle.

*She takes hold of the front of his overall and shakes him
vigorously backwards and forwards. Puts her face close to his
aggressively.*

BETTY. I'll tell you one of my little womanly secrets, shall I?
(*He nods.*) A little thing that rouses me? (*He nods.*) Something that floods me with warm passion and exposes me to
the will of another?

VAL. Hey up, don't go mad about it . . .

BETTY. It's: Why haven't we got a home!

VAL. Right in my ear.

BETTY. When are we going to get a home!

VAL. When I've cracked it with these mushrooms, Betty, you
know that. (*She stumps over to look in the mushroom-boxes.*)
I'm not having less than the best for you, Betty.

BETTY. Val, there aren't any mushrooms here.

VAL. Yes, dear, I know, and nor there weren't any yesterday . . .

BETTY. There haven't been any in all the six weeks we've been
here.

VAL. No, that's the curious thing. D'you think perhaps the
conditions aren't quite right?

BETTY. And supposing they did come up, what's that going to
help?

VAL. I'll have thousands upon thousands of spores of giant
mushrooms, that's what I'll have, my lovely wife.

BETTY. Giant.

VAL. Giant. Nine-inch mushrooms. Get your spores here; succulent, firm, tender. Give us a kiss, Betty.

BETTY. How d'you know they'll be giant?

VAL. They were damn big in our cellar, I can tell you.

BETTY (*getting wild*). Well, so why didn't you grow 'em in your cellar.

VAL. I did, I just told you.

BETTY (*crazy*). Val! Val!

VAL. I know what you're wondering.

BETTY (*paroxysms*). Val! Val!

VAL. I'll buy you a bungalow and everything, you see, only my Dad kept on getting up earlier than me and nicking them off so I couldn't ever get any spores. Don't make a row, Betty. (*She clutches her hand round her mouth.*) Aren't you going to ask me why not make a row? (*She shakes her head dumbly. He starts to tense up during the next few exchanges.*) You think I don't worry, don't you?

BETTY (*deep breath; on the edge of angry tears*). I don't *like* calling you and carping, you leather-headed clown: I'd much rather be in the barmy little world you set up, honestly.

VAL. Sorry, Betty, I know I'm a hard man.

BETTY. That you are; you're a flipping hard man for a wife to love. I mean, d'you know what you're at at all?

VAL. Yes, of course I do.

BETTY. What if we get caught, for instance?

VAL. Yes, yes, I do worry about that.

BETTY. I'm fed-up of eating in cafés. I'll get round-shoul-dered.

VAL. You'll be glad and proud when I've cracked it . . .

She registers that his tone has been coinciding less and less with his words and looks up at him. His head swivels round and up and then down to look at her again.

BETTY. You could smile.

VAL. It's him again.

BETTY. No, it isn't.

VAL. It was you making that row; he's on to us.

BETTY. Who is? (*Swift.*) No, I didn't mean to ask that! (*But
  it's too late:* VAL's *head swivels up with a galvanic yelp.*)

VAL. Him up there! (*Head down slowly again and controlled.*)

BETTY. I wish you wouldn't do that!

VAL. How can I help it?

BETTY. You don't even try.

VAL (*gestures to the coalfeeds*). He can't see down those.

BETTY. Of course he can't, you gawk!

VAL. Might do it by mirrors.

BETTY. It's jam-packed by coal!

VAL (*uncertain*). He's cunning. I bet he watches you go by,
  eh? Looks over the edge of the hopper.

BETTY. What d'you think?

VAL. Ankle-level. I wish you wouldn't come that way.

BETTY. I bet his wife has something better than yours has,
  anyway.

VAL. Oh? Oh yes?

BETTY. It'd serve you right if I stopped and had a chat with
  him one of these nights: I might ask *him* what *he* thought a
  husband ought to do to be a husband. I'd hint.

VAL. Chat. And then tell me about it afterwards.

BETTY. And then tell you about it afterwards.

VAL. I'd go raving mad.

BETTY. You might be persuaded to do something about your
  wife then.

VAL. Oh cripes, yes.

BETTY. And what about mornings?

VAL. Mornings?

BETTY. Supposing I was to chat on my way *out*? *After* I've
  left you, dreamboat?

VAL. I think we should have dinner together at the café as
  well.

BETTY. I'll have to remember that trimmer; he's done me one good turn, he might do me another.

VAL. I think you should know, Betty, that I'm an undifferentiated schizophrenic and an evasive personality with manifestations of primitive and sexual fantasies associated with hostility and gross evidence of paranoid thinking.

BETTY. Are you?

VAL. I think so, it's hard to tell if you are one.

BETTY. So what does that make me?

VAL. You being here, it's a whole lot better, don't you see? With me working nights: young married woman, newly awakened . . . at least I know where you are. I'm jealous, you know. Course I am. Red . . . hot-blooded. Scenes of raging jealousy. Raging scenes of jealousy. Jealous scenes of . . . (*He breaks off and does his silent whistle.*)

BETTY. I don't know what you think you've got against him when you haven't seen him. I've seen him and I've got nothing against him.

VAL. Against him. He'll get his. (*Gestures up and around excitedly.*) Scraping around up there without a harness. Who puts him up to it?

BETTY. How d'you know he hasn't got a harness?

VAL. If he wore a harness I'd hear him hook on to the edge of the hopper, wouldn't I? But no, thud I hear, and then shovel, shovel, *scrape*; which means him jumping down, shovelling a bit to fill up the hole where it dips in the middle, and then *fiddling about* waiting for the coal to go down. You know what it should be, don't you? It should be clink tug-tug, then scutter down shovel, then scutter up again . . .

BETTY. Yes, he wants to get up again quick out of there, doesn't he?

VAL. Dust.

BETTY. And somebody might be going by.

VAL. What's he doing hanging about like this? You know what'd happen if I speeded up the intake, don't you?

BETTY. I expect you'd get burning coal out at the waste chute instead of dust and clinker, wouldn't you?

VAL. I might get trimmer coming down the coalfeed an' all, mightn't I? (*She gapes.*) And then firebeater would have big chats with trimmer about who chats with who and about what and mind your business. I'd say, 'Don't you get hotheaded about it.' Oh yes, I would. I'd joke about it. In a bitter and superior sort of way.

BETTY. You wouldn't.

VAL. Oh, wouldn't I?

BETTY. No!

VAL. No, o' course I wouldn't, would I? He wouldn't fit. How big is he?

BETTY. So what you want to say it for?

VAL *climbs into the top bunk and lies down.*

VAL. I do my best.

MRS MURRAY *opens the door.* '*Sky at Night.*' BETTY *conceals herself smartly in the bottom bunk.* MRS MURRAY *comes over to the bunks and looks at* VAL *in the top one.*

MRS MURRAY. Brose? (*He doesn't stir.*) Please don't disturb yourself. Brose, it is now four fifteen in the morning, and if you think I like it you're wrong. However, I must warn you that your birds are coming home to roost. (*He is silent.*) Be quiet. For manifold reasons Mr Price *and* Mr Mort are coming down here; and dawn, Brose, is doom. The fact – I may have said this before – the fact that I know you to be an undifferentiated schizophrenic and an evasive personality with manifestations of primitive and sexual fantasies associated with hostility and gross evidence of paranoid thinking does not alter the fact that you are far and away the least satisfactory firebeater we have ever had. I'll go further, you are the least satisfactory person we've ever had. I'll go further – no I won't. I have arranged for your duties to be taken over by an ex-military policeman who has been dismissed the service of the Congolese Militia. I've come here early to tell you that I can no longer defend such . . . such . . . and the instantaneous sack is the best you can hope for. If I had my way you'd go before two commissioners in lunacy and a medical certificate: what possessed you to distribute those pamphlets ? What ? I've tried to be understanding, from the start, haven't I ?

VAL. What pamphlets ? I was never near them. There was one through my door.

MRS MURRAY. You were *seen* pushing them through doors. Mr Price's, the Vicarage . . .

VAL. There's a dangerous maniac about; might be a gang. Blackmail at the back of it I shouldn't wonder; they'll do anything.

MRS MURRAY. But why *me* ?

VAL. I thought it might stop you releasing my tensions and that. I got a right bonk on the nut. If you had that to worry about.

MRS MURRAY. 'Denton Dye Works Better Watch Out.'

VAL. Huh. And 'Not Pink with Dye But Red With Blood Shall the River Run.' I can't help being an idiot.

MRS MURRAY (*gritted teeth*). You're not an idiot.

VAL. Oh yes, I am.

MRS MURRAY. I'll tell you what you are. You are incapable of – you are not capable of anything – good gracious I'm at it again! I'm trying to help!

VAL. It's only polite, isn't it ?

MRS MURRAY. Is it ?

VAL. Oh yes. You see a bloke, for instance, with a jamjar full of toenail clippings on his mantelpiece and you say: 'What's those ?'

MRS MURRAY. What are they.

VAL. Toenail clippings.

MRS MURRAY. I know.

VAL. Oh, you knew already? Well, that just goes to show,
doesn't it? You don't even know the bloke and yet you don't
laugh at him. Nobody would. More likely say: 'Oh, yes?
How interesting.' And you find yourself having a big conversation about toenail clippings and their infinite variety.
For politeness.

MRS MURRAY (*shudder*). Toenail clippings.

VAL. Sort of thing you might get really fascinated in. Might
even get yourself one of those big sweet jars. And a small
pickle pot for swops.

MRS MURRAY (*repelled*). I suppose it's remotely possible.
From an atavistic point of view any parings from the body
contain some of the person's virtue, the subconscious might
respond.

VAL. The id.

MRS MURRAY. Yes, the id.

VAL. Latin: id, meaning 'that'. Hence 'id-iot', meaning 'that
idiot'. Also 'idio-tic': that twitching idiot.

MRS MURRAY. Idiocy's infectious.

VAL. I bet it is.

MRS MURRAY (*completely disorientated, she makes several
attempts to follow a consecutive line of thought, which results
in her mouth opening and shutting; does a silent whistle;
passes her hand over her brow*). I've . . . I've told you what
I came here to say: Nemesis approaches. If you value your
employment here at all you might (*a*) make some gesture in
the direction of diminishing the dense column of black
smoke that currently divides the night sky, (*b*) try another
guess or two at the phasing and pressure figures on your
time-sheet, possibly even look at the dials, (*c*) get out of bed.
Alternatively you could leave now; it would not make the
slightest difference. Good morning.

She waits for some response, but VAL *lies calm and still as ever. She moves sedately to the door.*

BETTY (*invisible*). What did she have to come in here for? I was just getting some sense out of him!

MRS MURRAY stops in her tracks, turns full circle and then accelerates for the door and goes. 'Sky at Night.' VAL judders rhythmically in his bunk for a moment. Imitates the clang of a ship's bell.

VAL. Dang-dang, dang-da.

Outside the light changes to day. VAL judders in the bunk, steadily, then quietly and without gesture or movement:

The night was deep, and solid. The Southern Cross
Was a faint sketch of light, and no moon.
The silent swell rose swiftly, plunged,
No ripple broke the glass mighty surface,
Only a feeling within the dark ship
As of a resistless current lifting and thrusting.
And the drowned captain dreamed of waiting reefs.

He sits up, struggling at his collar, gets down and looks in at the curtains of the lower bunk.

The native girl slept, open as a seal.
For a year she had not spoken, could she speak?
For a year he had sailed, keeping her close, his 'object',
And now the deep-sailing manta rays and the porpoise
Could see again the black hull sliding
And the reefs of her father's island were waiting for their
own.

He grabs the phone. Barks into it.

Bridge! Take soundings at first light, keep watch forrard.
Keep her on course, keep her south by east. (*Slams down the phone.*)

But even below he could feel the ocean moving
Feel the dark green pull and the racing reef.

(*Harshly to* BETTY.) I'm going on deck!

> *She sweeps back the curtain, uncurls and stands by the up-*
> *right of the bunk, posing, sure of her effect.*
> *The phone gurgles. He snatches it up and speaks without*
> *waiting:*

Keep her on course, swing her south by east!

> *He slams down the phone.*

The girl stood, soft and implacable, woman
And the warm oily iron beneath his feet
Told him the turning screw and the luminous wake
That curved and veered and would not answer her helm.

TANNOY (*magnified murmured aside*). There's summat up.
(*Crackle. Official.*) Calling boiler-room, calling boiler-room:
will the night stoker repeat his message, please? Will the
night stoker please go to the phone, please? Thank you.

VAL (*harsh*). I must go to the bridge. I must go to the bridge,
woman!

> *Back to narrative.*

The elbowing engines pummel the water and ahead
And ahead and ahead the white thundering water
Foams over the horizon, filled with spikes.

BETTY (*still, sombre*). I am Tondalao.

> *The phone belches urgently three times.*

VAL (*hoarse, urgent*). My little belter.
BETTY (*Mabel Lucie Atwell falsetto, recites*).

We are the enter-tainers, littel boys and girls.
(*Then sober, pain-streaked authority with long timed pauses:*)

You . . . take us . . . (*Correction.*) We give
Ourselves into your pleasure. What a . . . what
Insolence you show to watch us dance
On strings that cut dance on strings that cut.
We . . . I . . . I am not an instrument
NOT an instrument of your entitled delight.
You are not *allowed* to use me, I belong with my people
I belong.
And my difference from you is not your pleasure but my
Importance.

The phone belches urgently. Suddenly they both stagger as if the room has lurched. She clings to the bunks, he reels across to above her.

VAL. She's struck! She's struck! Tondalao, you she-devil!!

He takes a bucket of water and empties it carefully over her head. Replaces the bucket and then staggers across the room dramatically for a better view of her. She is standing, soaked and hands on hips, thinking of awful words.

Oh. (*Smirks. Half-sings:*)

And the captain said 'Yo-ho, my lads',
And they tied him to the rigging as the ship went down.

BETTY. You merry andrew, you.
VAL. No, don't you see? You have to have that. The native girl always gets soaking wet. Sorry, Betty, have my hanky. (PRICE, *carrying a rolled-up copy of 'The Times', followed by* MORT *and* MRS MURRAY, *enter to centre briskly. They contemplate the scene. After a moment:*) Pity you had to wear a bra, though; I don't think that's usual.
PRICE. At least he's up. (*To* BETTY.) You look smart; who got you ready? (*To* VAL.) Now then, Brose.
VAL. Of course, the thing is, all this happened yesterday.
MORT (*he knows the game*). And will it happen tomorrow?

VAL (*frightened*). It already has done.

MORT *goes to him and shakes him roughly.*

MORT. Pull yourself together, man. You are a man?

VAL. If you say so.

MORT. You know what happens to a man who goes creepy-crawling about?

VAL. I expect he gets a kick up the bum.

MORT. Well?

VAL *blinks at him.* MORT *takes him by the shoulders to the door, opens it – 'Chanson du Matin' – and boots him out. Shuts the door and comes back dusting his hands with satisfaction.* VAL *comes back in.* 'Chanson du Matin.'

VAL. I'll go, you know. You don't have to tell me twice.

MRS MURRAY. There's your cards.

VAL. Oh. Oh yes, nice.

PRICE. I'll give you credit, you've been a source of amusement. I think I'll collect you.

MORT. I can't stand jelly babies. What's he *for*? What's he about? (*To* VAL.) You realize you deserve to be dragged through the courts for clean air offences?

MRS MURRAY. Not to mention breach of contract. I think you might strike him, Mr Price, while on company land.

MORT. Wet worm. Wet worm. You know I don't believe he'd bleed?

PRICE. No flim-flam, Mr Brose?

VAL. No, thanks, I've just had one.

PRICE. I'm sorry, I thought you'd go on your way with some jest.

VAL. Oh, I'm not going, don't you worry; not even when you call me Mr Brose again. Not going just now.

PRICE (*roguish*). Oh yes, you are, aren't you?

VAL. Actually, no.

PRICE (*bursting with good humour*). We've made a mistake again, haven't we? We've got our jotters.

VAL. That's right; and look: seven stamps, that's nice to see.

PRICE. So we're off?

VAL (*anxious*). Actually no, not for a while.

MORT. Go.

VAL. No.

MRS MURRAY. Go.

VAL. No go.

PRICE. You – er, notice that I don't ask you to explain, eh?

VAL. Yes, I do. You didn't ask me about Betty either, and I had quite a good one about her: something along the lines of 'Miss Caroline Booth stood rigid, as from the touch of a torpedo'. With impressions. (PRICE *sniggers knowingly and unmelodiously*.) Nor you didn't ask me about the old mushrooms either. Nor the pamphlets. Because you *knew*.

PRICE. What's that?

VAL (*here it comes*). You were informed. (PRICE *nods his head, chuckling, but he won't ask*.) Someone told you about everything.

PRICE. I wonder who that might have been? (VAL's *head begins to swivel to the side and up*.) Don't answer that question. It was intended as a purely rhetorical . . .

VAL (*galvanic yelp*). Him up there!! (*Head swivelling down*.)

PRICE. Good God. (*Whacks* VAL *across the back of the neck with 'The Times'*. VAL *pitches head over heels and on to his feet again*.) Did you see that? (*Whacks* VAL *on the forehead*. VAL *drops backwards, bounces on his bum and up again at once*.) He's having me on. (*Whacks* VAL *on the top of the head*. VAL *doesn't move*.) No, I don't suppose there was much point in that.

MRS MURRAY. I should think it would make you feel better in yourself, Mr Price.

PRICE. Yes.

VAL. If you do that again, I shall go limp and offer no resistance.

MORT (*hand out for the paper*). Can I have a go?

MRS MURRAY. I think that'll do.

MORT (*taking off his jacket*). Well, for heaven's sake, you can't just *leave* him here! He's got to go; you've told him to. It's socially inefficient conduct. Put your fists up, you. (*To* VAL.)

MRS MURRAY. Mr Mort.

MORT. He makes me wild. (*To* VAL.) Put up your fists. (*Sizes up to* VAL.)

MRS MURRAY (*not unduly disturbed*). Believe me, I understand: but do not, I beg you, confuse a feeling of guilt at your need for conformity with your principles. (VAL *makes no effort to meet* MORT's *challenge.* MORT *pile-drives his right fist into* VAL's *midriff, sending him sprawling.*) The super-ego is not divine.

MORT. All I want to do is hit him; we'll work out a principle for it later. (*Picks up* VAL, *who teeters.*) Great heavens, what's *your* idea? We should take down the boilerhouse brick by brick from round him and re-erect it elsewhere? We'd find him inside when we'd done! He's sneaky. (*Sets* VAL *up for the knockout.*)

VAL (*weakly to* BETTY). Help.

BETTY. I'm just waiting for you to show what you're made of.

VAL. This. Help.

> MORT *sends a beautiful straight left to the jaw.* VAL *goes down like a stone.*

PRICE. That's the way to polish em off.

> MORT *puts on his jacket.*

MRS MURRAY (*inspired*). We should change the job.

PRICE. What? Go over to oil?

MRS MURRAY. No. Oh, what insecure animals men are: we can't get the job done properly: change the job.

PRICE. Like the Russians with their sentries?

MRS MURRAY. I've no idea, but do you know what you want?

PRICE (*intense*). I want steam, I want steam. I don't want black smoke, chintz curtains, women, mushrooms, pamphlets. I want high-pressure steam, steam, steam all the time, steam. (*Jumps on* VAL.)

MRS MURRAY ('*You're losing your tem-per*'). You want people to do as they're told, don't you?

MORT (*hotly*). Oh yes. Watch it, Price; this is where you're supposed to start feeling guilty.

PRICE. Well, I'm not! (*Jumps on* VAL *again*.) I feel fine. I work, don't I? I don't ask anybody to do anything I wouldn't do if I had to. I'm at it night and day! I see no benefit! I get no satisfaction from it!

MRS MURRAY. Then we shall have to see about changing your job, too, shan't we?

PRICE (*pop-eyed*). You do realize, don't you, that this is how crimes of passion are provoked?

MRS MURRAY. You know, I'm almost glad to be up and at work early. This specimen, (VAL, *still prone*.) inferior as he is, has provoked fruitful thought, don't you think? And these hidden pressures in all of us can be toxic.

MORT. Oh, he's done me good . . . He's definitely done me good. (*Rubs his hands*.) He's an example of the species, isn't he? Mm.

PRICE (*hauls* VAL *up*). How can you be sure?

MORT. It's the two legs mostly, and the opposed finger and thumb. (*Demonstrates*.) Show Mr Price.

VAL *does, feebly*.

PRICE. Say, 'Ah'.

VAL. All right, but I'm not dropping my slacks and coughing. (*Opens his mouth*.) Matter of fact, I can retract my uvula without saying 'Ah'. (*Opens his mouth again*.)

BETTY. Don't you dare say 'Ah'.

VAL. I didn't.

BETTY. Well, just don't you dare.

VAL. What's the matter, Betty?

BETTY. You . . . you . . . you . . . I'll best you, and I know how I'll do it, too. (*Marching to the door.*)

VAL. Don't go, Betty!

BETTY. You know where I'm going, don't you?

VAL. You've no business adding to my worries at a time like this.

BETTY. I'm going where I might find a man, aren't I?

VAL (*mutters*). Over the edge of the hopper . . .

BETTY. You know that.

VAL. I know that. Oh, yes. Only can't you see I'm busy?

MRS MURRAY. They're absolutely *real*, aren't they? Quite unselfconscious.

VAL. It's my mushrooms, you can understand that.

PRICE (*chortles*). It's his mushrooms.

BETTY. Standing there making holes with your fingers and thumbs and saying 'Ah'.

VAL. That was only to baffle them; I'm coldly determined, Betty, honestly.

BETTY. Tarah. I might come back. After.

VAL. What about my barmy little world?

BETTY. The trouble with getting inside your head is that once I'm there I'm on my own. (*She goes. 'Chanson du Matin.'*)

> VAL *is paralysed by distress. He goes blindly to the mush-rooms and gropes vaguely at the boxes. They have sprung into life and the top two boxes perch crazily on the abundant rubbery mauve caps. He fumbles unseeing among them and takes one.*

MRS MURRAY (*confidential*). Don't push it; let him stew. Whatever occurs to you to do, do the opposite.

> VAL *is taking the mushroom over to the cupboard, where he finds a small pan into which he crumbles the mushroom, adds some milk and then sets to cook on the slowly turning bars of the fire-box.*

PRICE. What about when the opposite occurs to us first?

MRS MURRAY. Do that.

PRICE. He's . . . he's . . .

MORT (*averting his eyes from* VAL *with an effort.*) I think I take Mrs Murray's point: his behaviour is not sequent, he's liable to do anything and everything, therefore the best we can do is to oppose his doing anything we want him to do . . . (*Faltering.*)

PRICE. Look what he's doing.

MORT. . . . recommend him to do what we don't want him to do, or possibly refrain from any action . . .

PRICE. He's stewing mauve toadstools, that's what he's doing.

MRS MURRAY (*strained*). He wants opposition. Very well let him make his own; that way he'll be less certain of it. What's he doing now?

PRICE. It'll be *felo de se*, you know – while the balance of the mind, eh? We can all subscribe to that, eh?

MORT. Might just make him ill.

MRS MURRAY. Every likelihood. I don't think I can bring myself to interfere. (VAL *fishes out a piece and eats it tentatively. They look the other way.*) Who knows but what events are coming your way, Mr Price? Mr Price.

PRICE. Balance of the mind – oh yes, but whose mind? D'you fancy giving a rough account of all this to a coroner?

MORT (*sidles over*). How're you getting on, Brose?

VAL (*dreamy*). All right.

MORT. Good man.

VAL. S'funny, I've just fulfilled an ambition, you realize that? I ought to be bouncing about, but I'm very calm.

PRICE. Er, can you see your life as a vast panorama?

VAL. Beatific. (*To* PRICE.) Put your hat on.

PRICE. I've got it on.

VAL. No, you haven't.

PRICE. Yes, I have. (*Checks.*) Anyway, don't tell me whether I should wear my hat or not, if you please. My hat.

VAL. Nude men should always wear a hat. (*Looks at* MRS MURRAY.) Doesn't matter so much with nude women.

MORT. We're not nude, you know, Brose.

VAL. Oh yes, you are – very.

All three are giving each other sneaky glances.

MORT. I don't think I can go through with this: the ethics are dubious, aren't they?

PRICE. Deep down in my bowels I have a feeling for him; it's hard to be exact, but I'd guess it's black hatred.

MRS MURRAY. A doctor, d'you think? Or an emetic?

VAL. I'd like to see Betty.

MRS MURRAY. Of course, of course.

VAL. Got a mole on her shoulder.

MRS MURRAY *claps a hand to her shoulder. Retracts the gesture. Accidentally arranges her hands to cover her modesty. Looks at the others.*

MRS MURRAY. It's just that I don't like to think about it. I think I'll go. That young lady will be wandering about.

PRICE. You're right; it's by no means safe.

MORT. D'you mind if I have a bite?

VAL. Go ahead. There'll be thousands, tell your friends.

MORT. I'll settle this. (*To* VAL.) From an entirely scientific viewpoint. (*Takes and eats a piece.*) There. Actually they're rather nice, mushroomy.

VAL. A good nine inches, eh?

MORT. Oh yes. (*To the others.*) Try a bite.

MRS MURRAY. I'm sure I don't want to come near.

PRICE. They're . . . good, are they?

MORT *is staring at* MRS MURRAY.

MORT. Mm? Oh yes, excellent. The milk is a nice touch.

PRICE. No ill effects at all?

MORT. There is a slight . . . (*Shakes his vision clear.*) I do detect an infusion of warmth.

MRS MURRAY. I'm going to find that girl. (*She goes out side-ways.* '*Chanson du Matin.*')

MORT. Mrs Murray! I trust my . . . (*To* PRICE.) I hope my scientific and detached gaze was not misinterpreted by Mrs Murray?

PRICE. Give us a try of that stuff, Brose.

> VAL *gives him a bit.*

MORT. She's a very fine woman, don't you think?

PRICE (*gulping down*). You're joking. D'you mean you really saw her . . . well – er, er . . . mm, not bad. I think I'll just try one more piece.

MORT. Mr Price, I don't know what you take me for. (PRICE *grins at him and sniggers.*) Some sort of mild toxicant. Hazes the vision to a . . . a pinkishness. That's the shade, mm. And a pleasing drowsiness.

PRICE (*souring*)' Doesn't affect me. (*Sideways glances at* VAL *and* MORT. *Takes* VAL *by the ear. Cold.*) You'll finish this week out, d'you hear?

VAL. All right.

PRICE. Right.

VAL. I wish everyone wouldn't keep changing their mind. Still, if that's what you want. I want everyone to have their heart's desire.

PRICE. That's what *I* want. And you're a right one to talk about everyone changing their minds.

VAL. Why, wasn't it my turn?

MORT (*away*). A feeling not unlike . . . in my undergraduate days. Oh, glorious rubbery legs. (*To* VAL.) Shake hands, no hard feelings.

VAL (*shaking hands*). You've got a handy left.

MORT. Oh, that was kind.

PRICE. Coming, parson?

VAL. Never mind, Mr Price, perhaps it'll take longer to work with you.

MORT (*sings*). 'Jolly good gloating weather . . .' (*Beams at* VAL *and* PRICE.) Two pink persons. You're both pink.

PRICE (*stares blearily*). So are you. Oh – er, em, d'you think we should go and find Mrs Murray now? I feel rather cheerful in mood. I'll tell her some jokes. (*To* VAL.) I did get my own way, didn't I, eh?

VAL. That's right.

MORT. Are your legs rubbery?

PRICE. I'm not sure. They're down there somewhere. Have a feel if you want.

> They smile radiantly at each other. Then MORT throws a comradely arm round PRICE and they both make for the door on rubbery legs.

MORT. Hot in there, isn't it?

> They go. 'Chanson du Matin.' VAL squats, beatific. Thud on the loose coal above. The boiler is beginning to glow red. Languidly VAL swivels his head up to look. Thud. Pause. Thud. ALY comes belting in. 'Chanson du Matin.'

ALY. I protest! The rhythm of my work is greatly disturbed in the 'oppers. Greatly greatly. (*Sees* VAL. *Approaches.*) No more persons must come down here up there. (*Examines* VAL.) Do you see beyond life?

VAL. No.

ALY. You do not comprehend life in its totality?

VAL. No.

ALY. Excuse me, you seem to be in a trance-like condition. Do you assure me that you see nothing?

VAL. Yes.

ALY. I wonder why that should be?

VAL. I've got this bad eyesight.

ALY (*sighs*). I shall never know what is God. How can you have a whole small country with no mystical experience except dominoes and Guinness?

VAL. God is a circle whose centre is everywhere and its circumference nowhere.

ALY. You may be right.

The steam-valve begins to blast off. VAL *twiddles a few knobs without looking and the boiler subsides.*

A very fine-looking young lady has come into my 'oppers for a discussion. As a result of what she said I told her of my great love and offered her a position in one of my luxurious houses. Let us shampoo each other, I said.

VAL. That's my wife. Betty she's called.

ALY. The work was of a most proper and cleanly kind. Receptionist. I beg your pardon. However, Mr Price and the others followed shouting and laughing joyfully in my 'opper, and our arrangements were interrupted. This is why I was angry. Do not worry now.

Various clanks, poppings and grindings come from the boiler.

VAL. Hey, you want to try one of those mushrooms. I'm a made man from this out.

ALY (*tries one*). Are you sure that is the correct way to control the boiler?

Cloink from the boiler.

VAL. Go on, have a twiddle.

ALY *does so, with glee.*

ALY. Oh joy. (*Chewing.*) My dear old fellow, these are most delicious. And a deeply splendid and significant size in original condition.

The controls blow up. VAL *folds his rubbery legs to sit and waves* ALY *to sit facing him: pupil and sage.*

VAL. D'you like happy endings?

ALY. Oh yes.

Cloink cloink kerr, from the boiler.

VAL. Bedtime story.

ALY. O.K.

VAL. And they all lived happily ever after.

ALY. Who did?

VAL. Mr Mort, who drew one-all with the secret dragons; Mr
Price, who shall remain nameless.

ALY. Very fine.

Grind grind grind and an appalling screech from the boiler.

VAL. Mrs Murray, who shall be lusted after but untouched.

ALY. O.K.

VAL. And Betty, who has found her prince.

ALY (*demurs*). I prefer Mahatma as a title.

VAL. And once upon a time . . .

*A prolonged reverberating boom from the boiler as it
collapses, spewing its steam, smoke, soot and coal.*

There was a boiler. Once upon a time.

And the play is over

AMERICAN CENTURY SERIES